The Fragrance

OF A RESILIENT

Woman

Different scents of victory from resilient women...

Collaborating Authors

The Fragrance

OF A RESILIENT

Woman

Published by:

B&B Publishing and Co.

www.garbuniversity.com

Contact: 469-632-6384

Table of Contents

A scent of Encouragement

By

Ashalee Nelson

During the times we experience hardships, we may feel as though it will never come to an end. The heartache from the present situation or situations from our past may hinder our wellbeing. I want you to hold on to God's unchanging hand. His word says, "He will never leave nor forsake you."

As a child, I experienced tough times that led me to learn how to trust in God. I was the firstborn of a teenage girl who was lost in this world. She left her mom's home at the age of 15 years old, pregnant with her first child. She was trying to figure out her purpose in life and raise a baby of her own. She moved in with a family who helped her until she was able to get her life in order. After giving birth to me, she moved in with my godmother who was a cousin by marriage.

As time went by, she had two more kids, which was a more challenging situation during her early 20's. As a toddler, I can remember my biological mom experiencing stressful situations. A young parent not knowing what to do in certain conditions with raising three kids, she lived with a cousin by marriage. Being a young parent, I could imagine the immaturity to care for three kids while trying to make a living and find a home to call your own. She was abusive to me as the oldest who had the responsibility to care for my younger siblings. I cannot recall every situation, but I can remember this one time of getting whipped with an extension cord for not doing what I should have done.

As time went by, the young mother of three kids would go out to party often. She left her kids with people who she thought to be her friend at the time. The word was out that her friend was inappropriately touching her son. Friends and family were concerned for the three kids, then soon this all came to an end. Three kids were taken away from their mother and separated. The child protection service sent them to other family members at the ages of 5, 2, and a few months old. I was a toddler receiving a monitored visit from our mother through child protection service. She tried to get us back but was not successful. As the oldest of the three kids, I was the one my mother tried to get back because she believed; she could care for me at that age. I felt lost, alone, angry at a young age, dealing with this situation the best way I knew. At the time, I did not know where my siblings were. I was placed with my Aunt and Uncle, who had four daughters of their own. I can remember having temper tantrums, not understanding what happened to my mother and brothers. A child living with people who loved her, but they were not her own. This feeling can cause a child to act out in a way an adult would not understand. I found myself feeling as though the world was against me. I wished to know where my mother was. Things were getting hard for my Aunt as her four daughters grew older, and they began to have kids of their own.

Eventually, I was placed with my godmother who had no kids at the time. She was a caring person with a great sense of humor. She was known for fun to hang out with by her cousins. I was excited to move in and have someone to call my own. Although I felt as though I was with someone to call my own, I continued to have dreams about the first time I had ever seen snow. A strange man in a truck took us away from our mother. I continued to wonder, where are my siblings? We started to have monitored visitations with our mother. At the time, I would get to see my two brothers. Gradually, the visit became less often, and then no more visits at all. Although I was with people who loved me, there is nothing like receiving love as a child from your mother. "No love like a mother's love."

My mother eventually gave up on trying to get her kids back. I can remember her saying, "family was against me." She had a job, her home, and still, nothing was enough to get her kids back. It was years and no contact from my biological mother. Then she called that she was in prison. I can remember the times she called from jail, crying and asking for my forgiveness. My mother was a sweet person. She would sing songs to me over the phone, such as the soft voice of a loving person. My mother was an amazing person to others. She was what you call, no good for her. I believe that not having her kids was a part of her wrong decision to care for herself. I cannot imagine how I would be without my kids; they are my world.

My godmother was fun to be around. Everyone enjoyed her company. Living with her was a joy as being the only kid at the time. A couple of years went by and she has her miracle baby, such a joy to have a sibling to call my own. I was a big sister!

As time went by, I became the child who had to take care of things around the home on my own. My godmother who became my stepmother had to work to provide for her two kids. At the age of nine years old, I learned to cook, clean, and care for the household. I began to feel like the slave of the home. I was no longer feeling the love I had in the past. I went back to feeling alone and no one to call my own. Keep in mind; I was not with my biological family. There is no love like the love from your mother and father as a child. I never knew how that felt. My stepmother had a husband that I do not have good memories of him. He did not help her around the way she needed, and the load became heavier for her. She had to work two jobs to make ends meet. As time went by, I started experiencing abuse from my stepmother. I did not understand what the reason was for being abused. It felt as though I was lost and confused with no hope. Being told, I could not do anything right while taking care of a home as a never taught child. My stepmother began to beat me more often. If I did not take care of the chores the correct way, it was a beating received. It started with a belt. Then it turned in to use of a wooden broomstick, a plastic toy bat, a wood stick as to anything she could get her hands on. I became afraid to make a mistake.

As the months passed by, I had to stay alone while my stepmother was working and started to have experiences with my stepfather that I did not understand. I can remember playing hide and seek games that required him to touch me in a way that made me uncomfortable and being unsure of it at the same time. I thought that was the love shown, and I was excited to receive love from a male figure finally. As a child, there were sexual relations with my stepfather. I can remember the event happening, but I cannot remember the exact time as I buried it away as I got older in hopes never to bring it up again. There was a shame as I blamed myself because I allowed it to happen and never told anyone. As a teenager, there was a feeling that I could not trust anyone. I was being the kid labeled as the troublemaker, disrespectful, and angry to the family around us. I did not have a voice and I was embarrassed. Imagine living in a world where you are dependent on the people who look at you as a terrible child. How could you trust others when the people who were supposed to love and take care of you betrayed you?

I began staying over at my great-grandmother's home. Great grandmother was getting older and needed someone to care for her, mainly at night. I love great grandmother! She taught me how to cook, clean, and spoke wisdom into me. There was nothing like receiving words from the wise. Great grandmother lived at the corner of our family church, and she made sure I knew the Lord. We went to church together, and I had to attend Sunday school as well. I never wanted to leave to return home. At home, there was physical abuse from my stepmother and sexual abuse from my stepfather that continues to go through my head. When my stepmother would put stepfather out, I would be relieved, but the beating was worst as I was the one she took her stressed out. I can remember her beating me outside in front of people who would verbalize to stop but never stopped her. I wished an adult would have stopped her when they saw her do it. I knew I could not talk to an adult when they watched me get beaten and never stood up for me.

I would love to attend church with a great grandmother, and I learned about God. I knew how I could always trust in him no matter what it is that I go through. As a child, I made sacrifices to God and prayed throughout the day. I asked him to protect me from the people I was living with because I lived in fear as a child. I can remember being terrified of doing anything wrong because I would get beaten for making a mistake. I was never taught how to do it but received a beaten for it. As I continued to stay with my great grandmother at night, I enjoyed it because it gave me peace of mind. As time went by, I found a closer relationship with God. Making sacrifices as I would experience the trauma as a child and hope someday I would overcome this situation. I can remember knowing because I took care of great grandmother saying God would bless me in return. I love to care for older people. Helping people when I could, and it came from my heart.

As the years went being a teenager in high school, there were insecurities in me, but at the time, I did not realize it. The beating continued during my high school and the inappropriate conversations from my stepfather. I can remember an aunt calling my stepmother and said your husband better not be putting his hands on my niece. I felt a relief that someone knew, and maybe it would stop. I wondered how she even knew because I never told anyone. That was the work of God, my thoughts. No one came to my rescue, and I continued to live there in fear. Eventually, after meeting this guy in high school, I was opened to him and let him know the way

I lived for years. He started to see the bruises on my body and was concerned for my safety. I can remember the time he said that I should not return home. It did not make any sense that someone would beat on a child this way. He never knew about the things that my stepfather did to me. That was not easy to speak about. As I grew older, I became tired of experiencing abuse. Enough! I ran away from home.

I was a senior in high school, close to becoming a dropout. I was determined to continue my last semester and graduate. I lived with the guy I met in high school and I was blinded by love. I always wanted to be loved by someone. The cheating began and I stayed through it. I did not leave thinking I finally had someone to call my own. I could not lose him. I continued to stay because I had found a job and worked to get on my feet and find my place to live one day. It is a wonder how people will see that you're in a situation where you need them and take that situation to their advantage and continue to bring you down even more. Finally, I was able to find a home that was affordable after working and saving my weekly paychecks. The guy from high school moved in with me and the cheating continued. I found myself going through heartache and pain, finding out, and fighting different women. I told myself that I was looking for love in the wrong places. I was seeking to find the love that I was missing as a kid in a man. I left the relationship then found myself taking him back. Not long after, I became pregnant, and then I felt I could never leave him. I did not want my child to grow up without her father the way I did. During my pregnancy, it was the worst. He stayed out late nights, alcohol, and fights. I had enough. Get out! I made up my mind I would not raise my child in this environment.

I had my daughter and applied for grants to help with tuition assistance. Since I was a single parent with low income, I was approved for assistance. I began turning to God the way great grandmother taught me. I began attending church again, working two full-time jobs to provide for my daughter. While in college, I met this young man. I had been through a lot in my life and I was not looking for a relationship with anyone. We would talk only at times we would meet on campus. It felt good talking to someone after experiencing this trauma in my life. As the months went by, we began having a conversation on the phone. One day we decide to go out on a date and then we kept in touch from then on. I was not in a committed relationship as I was taking care of my daughter and finding me. I did not trust anyone being around her because of how I was treated in the past. I protected her with all I had inside. As I continued to work on my career, I continued to form a closer relationship with God. As I kept the faith and sought God first, he continued to make a way out of no way. He placed all the people I needed in my life to help me to get to the next chapter. Gradually, I learn to love and trust again. I continued to keep in touch with the guy I met in college. We eventually started helping each other. My heart began to heal from past trauma. I did everything I could to make sure he was a better person because he was a part of me becoming a better person. God sent him just when I did not know how to love or trust again.

As the years went by, I became a Registered Nurse with a bachelor's degree. Currently, continuing my education as a graduate student. We have two additional girls to our family, and we are happily married. I had lost hope for a long time. I thought I found love after being abused mentally, physically, and sexually. I was insecure and allowed people to take advantage of me. Now, with the Lord on my side, I walk with my chest out and my head held high because I made it. Statistically, I should not have made it this far. This is only the beginning of what God has in store for me. Seek God in all things and he shall direct your path. I had some hardships since I was a child, but I am using it to tell my story to help someone who believes they have no way out. Stay encourage, go through it, and God will see you through. Be Blessed!

Getting to know Ashalee Nelson

Ashalee Nelson is the author of A Woman Lost in her Childhood (2020). She has a background as an educator, president, leadership role, and volunteer in her community. She is a registered nurse who has a passion for helping others. Ashalee shows empathy to those who trust in her with their issues. She wants to share her story to encourage others. She states it is a process to become the person you are destined to be in life. For years, many people have turned to Ashalee for comfort and advice. She is a motivation to others, and they wish to know how she does it. Ashalee says, "There have been trials, but I have a testimony."

Website: www.ashaleenelson.com

A Scent of Forgiveness

By

Jennifer Johnson

Everyone is on a journey called life. It may not be the same, but each journey is sure to offer personal and spiritual growth, which is needed to achieve one's fullest potential. Know that God predetermined our destiny and ordered the course of events to take place in our life.

I use to walk around carrying shame for things I've done, decisions I made, and situations I put myself in, leaving me to search for the light at the end of the tunnel. I did not understand why things were not going according to my plan. Indeed, each situation has taught me that I needed to learn how to move out of the way, stop fighting, and let God work in my life.

I learned never to confuse a season for a lifetime because everything has an expiration date. Seasons do not last forever; they are forever changing. Each season is meant for planting, watering, fertilizing, and blossoming. It was spring when I was able to blossom with grace.

Summer

The seed was planted in 1980 in Lakeview, New York (Long Island). You will never be able to convince me that there was a better block than Lafayette Avenue. I lived in the same house that my mom and her siblings grew up in and went to the same schools. Most of my friend's parents went to school with either my mom, aunt, or uncles. Everyone on the block (and in the neighborhood) knew each other. Whenever a child got in trouble, and an adult on the block witnessed it, best believe your parents knew about it before you got home. I was one of those kids. Mainly because my parents would tell me to stay on the block, but I wanted to follow the older kids and go where they went.

Summertime was the best. We didn't have video games, internet, air conditioning, computers, or cell phones. Just hot summer days with sunflower seeds, bike riding, double dutch, corner store runs, freeze tag, and water fights. We were outside playing all day until the street lights came on and sometimes longer if our parents were still outside with us.

Those were the days when I thought I knew everything and tried to be this perfect little girl. I could not wait to be an adult so I could make my own decisions. I had my whole life planned out. I was going to go away to an HBCU, then law school, move to New York City, become a lawyer, fall in love, get married, buy a house, have four children, and live happily ever after. They say God laughs when you make plans. I guess he was having a chuckle at my expense because my plan failed before I even started.

During my freshman year of high school, my parents decided to move to Virginia Beach, Virginia. I was devastated. I would be leaving all I'd ever known only to move to a state I visited once. I sulked the whole drive from New York to Virginia Beach in my mother's tan Chevrolet Chevette. My little brother was five at the time and sat in the back seat without a care in the world. However, I was not ready for this change, but I had no choice or a say so in the matter.

The most significant change in my life was having a baby at the age of 15. I was in the tenth grade and not ready to be a mother or handle the responsibility that came with it. I was still a young girl with a lot to learn. I knew I had to tell my parents I was pregnant, but was afraid. It's funny now, but it wasn't back then. My mother is a coffee drinker. Every morning without fail, she would make coffee. So, I got the idea to write a note telling her I was pregnant and leaving it in her coffee container to find the next morning.

I woke up the next morning, which was a Saturday, to the smell of coffee brewing. There was no turning back. I braced myself for what was to come. I walked downstairs into the kitchen. She gave me that mama look like we need to talk, and we did. I could see the disappointment in her face. Amid our conversation, I thought someone has to tell my father, but it wouldn't be me. I let my mother have that discussion with him.

After my mother broke the news to my father, I was called to my parent's bedroom to talk to him. I remember sitting on a cedar chest in front of the window. My father was sitting on the bed across from me. To this day, I can still recall the words he spoke to me. He told me that taking care of a baby is not easy at any age, but I was still a child. He said if I had my baby, I would end up like the girls who lived down the street in Friendship Village, with no education and living on the system. I wasn't expecting my father to jump for joy after hearing that his 15-year old daughter was pregnant, but I wasn't expecting him to count me out either. That day I made a promise to myself that I was going to prove him wrong and anyone else who thought like him.

I had no clue how I would take care of this baby, finish high school, and still achieve the goals I had for myself. I was already a statistic, and giving up was not an option. I couldn't fail. No matter what anyone's opinions were of me and my situation, I had to take care of my son and make sure he had the best life possible. It was my responsibility to take care of him and I did just that. I worked full time during the day, went to school at night, and graduated high school. Being a single teen parent was not something I expected but it happened. I was doing the best I could with what I had. I felt alone like no one understood my struggle, and I was tired of doing everything myself. I felt drained from working all day and going to school at night. Yet, I continued to push through and do what I needed to do. After graduating from high school, I began experiencing anxiety and depression. I was unsure of where I was going in life, consumed with fear and doubt.

One night I laid in bed thinking about my life. Every negative thought crept into my mind. I even contemplated taking my own life. I was struggling with depression and wanted to be at peace. Then I thought about the innocent life, my son, who was lying beside me—the toddler who loved me regardless of my failures. I looked at him as he slept peacefully. Tears welled up in my eyes and began to fall down my face. The longer I stared at him, the harder I cried. I thought if I were to take my own life, I would be leaving my son without a mother. I would be abandoning him, just like his biological father. I couldn't do that to him.

I pulled the covers off of me. I got out of bed and dropped down to the floor on my knees. I cried and prayed for God to help me. To take the negative thoughts out of my mind and give me the strength to keep going. I so desperately needed God to show me that everything was going to work itself out. I prayed that I would find my way and that God would bring someone into my life. Someone who I could connect with on a level that I never experienced before. Someone who I could talk to about any and everything, someone who would love my son and me and not judge my faults and failures. After praying and pouring my heart out to God, I got up off the floor and back into bed.

That night I had a dream that felt so real. I was in my car, driving to pick someone up. I pulled up to an apartment building. A man was standing outside wearing a white t-shirt, blue jeans, white sneakers, and a red baseball cap. I could not see his face, but I remember his physique; tall, dark, and slim. We sat in my car, talked, and laughed. It was such a peaceful dream.

Fall

I took a part-time job in the evening cleaning bathrooms at the Virginia Beach Central Library. I was still working full-time during the day but needed the extra money to move out of my parent's house. One evening I walked into the office to sign in for my shift. A guy walked in behind me. I proceeded to sign in and turned to walk out of the small office. Before I could make it out the door, I heard the guy say, "So, you're the infamous Jennifer." I was known as "infamous Jennifer" because some nights, I would sign in for my shift then leave without doing any work. After getting in trouble for doing that, I had no choice but to sign in and work. I didn't respond to his wisecrack. I was tired from working all day and tending to my son.

While cleaning the bathrooms, I would be in the zone, plotting my next move in life. I kept to myself and did my job. I knew the sooner I finished, the quicker I could get home. I walked out of the bathroom one night and was startled when I saw the guy who called me "infamous Jennifer" and his brother sitting on a bench across from the bathroom I was cleaning.

We laughed it off. Then he questioned why I stayed to myself and would always leave as soon as I finished cleaning. I explained that I was a single parent working two jobs. He proceeded to ask if I wanted to hang out with him sometime. I was shocked by his gesture because most guys didn't want anything to do with females in my situation. They assumed that there was baby daddy drama or didn't want to deal with the responsibility associated with dating a single mother. I agreed and gave him my pager number. I did not have a cell phone back then, just a pager.

A few days later, I got a page from a number I did not recognize. I called the number back. It was him asking if I wanted to hang out. I agreed and drove to his apartment to pick him up. I pulled up to his apartment. It felt like déjà vu. He was standing outside his apartment wearing a white shirt, blue jeans, white sneakers, and a red baseball cap. The same thing the guy in my dream was wearing. I genuinely believe that some dreams make you never want to go back to sleep, while others make you feel like you are on top of the world. However, the best dreams are fairy tales that come to life. He was my fairytale that came to life.

That night we went to the movies and came back to his apartment. We sat in the living room on the couch. We talked, laughed, and joked until almost 4 a.m. I felt a connection with him that night. There was something about his smile and his eyes that made me feel safe. Most guys I had been out with would've tried to have sex, but he was different. He was a true gentleman and didn't try anything. We were content talking and learning about each other.

We started spending more time together. I introduced him to my son, and they connected and established a bond. I introduced him to my family. They made it seem like he was already part of the family. Everyone loved him. It's weird because when we first met, I never thought I would marry him. But he became my best friend and so much more. He supported and encouraged me when I decided to go back to school. I graduated from college and started a career as a paralegal working in a law firm. We got married, had two daughters, and purchased our first home. I supported him when he decided to join the Army.

Like being a teen mom, our marriage proved to be another test for me, especially being a military spouse. We were 21 years old and still had a lot of growing up to do. I learned that marriage is like a flower. It won't grow if you forget to water it. I knew there would need to be compromise and communication in our marriage, but compromise wasn't always as simple as it seemed. My husband would tell me that I had a spirit of always wanting to be in control. I have to admit that was true. That stemmed from me being a single mother. I had no choice but to be responsible and to take control of my life. I had to make things happen for my son and I to survive. I also knew the goals I had for myself and strived to achieve them.

Early on in our marriage, I began feeling unappreciated as a wife. I thought I was doing everything a wife should do for her husband. I cooked, cleaned the house, took care of the children, and was supportive of my husband. But it never felt like it was enough for him. Don't get me wrong, he was a hardworking man and would help with the children, but he still wanted to hang out late with his friends instead of spending time with his family. I expected more from him. I needed more from him.

Fast forward a couple of years. We were down to one income. Daycare was like paying a mortgage, especially with two toddlers. We could no longer afford daycare, so I had to quit my job. We started falling behind on bills, even our mortgage and lost our home to foreclosure. The whole situation put more stress on our marriage. It made me feel like we were failures.

On the day of the foreclosure, I got a phone call from our mortgage company. The man on the phone told me if I wasn't at the courthouse trying to save my home, I needed to start packing because I was about to lose it. I hung up the phone, grabbed the yellow pages, and looked for a storage unit to store our belongings. The plan was to stay with my parents to save some money and find a new place. I felt the opposite of accomplished. I suddenly found myself further away from where I wanted to be—moving my family in with my parents. I was frustrated because of our situation and the distance between my husband and I was growing.

Finally, I found a new job and a better daycare situation for our girls. We were able to find a townhouse and move out of my parent's house. I was excited to get back in our own space. I tried to stay positive and trust that everything was going to be better. Right before we moved into our townhouse, I learned that my husband would be deploying to Iraq. The kicker for me was that he signed up to go, and he would be deploying with a different unit. He thought that deploying would help us financially.

Three days after we moved into our new place, he left for Iraq. I was home trying to handle my emotions—the feeling of failure for losing our home to foreclosure, frustration for having to quit my job, a career I worked hard to get into, and the daycare issue. Again, I felt like a single mother, lonely, unappreciated, and tired. I wanted an outlet for my feelings but went about it the wrong way. I did something that I never thought I would do. I cheated on my husband. I slept with another man. Something I thought could be a friendship turned out to be a physical and emotional affair that I tried to keep from my husband.

When my husband returned home from Iraq, he found out about my infidelity. I was sure he was going to want a divorce, so I prepared myself for that response. Figured I would be okay because I already felt like a single mother of 3, doing everything by myself while he was away. To my surprise, he didn't want a divorce. He wanted to work on our marriage, which we tried to do.

Winter

Fast forward four years. I sensed something different in our marriage. The distance was growing between us—something I should have questioned but didn't. We no longer had that connection we once had where we would talk, joke, and laugh with each other. I kept thinking things would get better over time, but they didn't. Then came New Year's Eve 2012. We decided to stay home and bring in the new year as a family, just the five of us. A few hours before the ball was to drop, my husband and I were sitting in our bedroom watching TV. Something in my spirit told me to ask him if he cheated on me. After I asked, there was a deafening silence in the room. I automatically knew what his response was going to be.

I tried to keep my composure and not get too loud because our children were in their bedrooms. That didn't last long. "She had a baby," he said. A scream bellowed out of me and through the house, causing my children to worry and panic. I couldn't let them see me in my anger. So, I left the house before I did something I would regret or end up in jail. I grabbed my phone and keys and ran out of the house before he could stop me. I was driving, and the tears kept coming. It became difficult for me to see the road. So many thoughts were going through my mind. Why was this happening? What would this news do to our children? Was it karma for me because of my infidelity? To make matters worse, we were in the process of purchasing a home and scheduled to close in two weeks.

I was finally able to pull myself together and get back home in time to bring in the new year. I walked through the door and could feel the tension in the house. I couldn't look at my husband's face because I knew it would intensify my anger. My focus was on bringing in the new year with my children. We toasted to 2013. I kept thinking that 2013 was already off to an atrocious start. Sadly, it would get worse before it got better. Before going to bed, I told my husband that all I wanted from him was for the closing of the house to go through, then he could go about his business. He nodded but didn't utter a word, which was smart. I glanced at his face. He looked like he knew this was the end of us.

That night, I tossed and turned and cried. I felt betrayed, hurt, and humiliated. I kept questioning whether I should stay or go. Only one person knew what was going on. I am so thankful for her friendship, her being there for me in my time of need, and not passing judgment on the situation. I refused to tell anyone else what was going on. I needed to pray about my situation and make a decision for myself and my children. For two weeks, I prayed, journaled, and cried. My husband, on the other hand, tiptoed around my emotions. He would ask what I was thinking about because I was moving in silence. He tried to make it clear that he wanted us to work things out. Of course, there was an apology and the backstory. How it hurt him to come home from deployment and learn that I cheated. That he thought I was still in communication with that same man, and it angered him. He felt the distance between us just like I did, but we both stayed silent about it instead of talking to each other. Two wrongs don't make a right. But none of that mattered at that point because the damage was already done.

I thought about the vows we said to each other before God, friends, and family. Vows that we both broke. I thought I would spend the rest of my life with this man. But he hurt me too bad to stay. They say, hurt people, hurt people and I didn't want to hurt anymore or hurt anyone else. I tried to look past my hurt and move forward with love and grace. I thought about forgiveness and how important it was for me to forgive so that I could move forward in my life. But would I forgive and stay or forgive and file for divorce?

Finally, I decided to forgive my husband and stay. Once the news broke about the infidelity and the child, I would hear, "you're a better woman than me" or "that couldn't be me." The truth is you never know what you can handle until you are put to the test. That is why I took time for myself, prayed, and made my own decision. Other people's opinions didn't matter to me and still don't. For me, it wasn't about being the better woman. It was about looking at the person and not their mistake. There were so many other things about him that were the deciding factor in my decision to stay.

I observed how empathetic he was for hurting me the way he did. I thought about our children and how much of a great father he is. He was a provider and protector. I knew he loved me. He just had a lapse in judgment, and our marriage paid the price. He showed me by his actions that he wanted our marriage to work. Forgiveness did not come easy. Sometimes a vindictive spirit would creep up on me. I would pray about it; God would show me that He is in control. All I had to do is sit back and watch Him work.

Me forgiving my husband meant that I would need to forgive the other woman. My husband was the one that broke his vow to me, but she played a role in all of it. I also had to be okay with being a step-parent. I was unsure whether or not I would be able to handle having this little boy in our home. It wasn't easy, but regardless of how I felt, there was an innocent child involved. He didn't ask to be born into this situation. I did know that I needed to give this little boy the same love, affection, and attention I give to my children and I did just that.

Sometimes in marriages, we become so consumed with work, kids, bills, and the household. We forget that our spouse needs to fit somewhere. We stop communicating our wants and needs with each other. My husband and I were both consumed with and about the wrong things. I felt unappreciated and abandoned, which led to my physical and emotional affair. The hurt from my affair led to his infidelity. We forgot to pay attention to the needs of each other. We stopped communicating with each other, and the trust was gone. It took therapy and having open and honest conversations to make it through. Above everything else, we had to bring God into our marriage. The devil tried to destroy our marriage and our family. Putting God first was the only way our marriage would survive.

Spring

As time passed, I became consumed with taking care of everyone else and burying every experience I had been through instead of healing from it. I felt mentally and physically drained. There is a saying that "God doesn't give you more than you can handle," but I was beginning to think he had gone overboard with me, and I was about to explode.

It's important to pay attention to your dreams because they can tell you a lot about yourself and reveal hidden secrets. I had no choice but to pay attention after a dream I had one night. I call it my soul awakening dream. I was sleeping but awoke to see a shining light at the top of the stairs in my dream. I got up, walked towards the stairs, and heard a compassionate yet powerful voice say, "if you are ready to come home, just keep on walking." I looked around, but it was only me standing with the white light shining bright in front of me. I heard the voice again, "if you are ready to come home, keep on walking towards the light." At that moment, all I could think about was my children and responded, "I can't leave my children." What I heard next, I felt in my soul. "Trust in me and everything will be okay. You don't have to carry everything...let it go". I woke up from that dream and cried my heart out. I know that voice was nothing but God.

I neglected to make myself a priority. I was striving for perfection and afraid to fail, putting other people's wants and needs over my own. I needed professional help and started therapy a few days later. My therapist helped me tackle my emotions. She also helped me see that I was blooming in grace. That God had used every situation I ever experienced for me to grow in grace. He bestowed upon me undeserved favor, a sacrificial gift that I had not earned and could never repay.

My therapist also pointed out something that never crossed my mind. She told me that I was quick to forgive and show compassion to others who hurt or disappointed me, but I never forgave myself. Instead of forgiving myself, I beat myself up about my mistakes and choices I made because they were not considered perfect behavior. It took me a minute to grasp what she was telling me because I never thought I needed to forgive myself for anything. She told me that I needed to forgive myself for some stuff and release it in order to move forward in life. But only I knew what needed to be forgiven and it required me to take time to figure it out for myself.

There was the shame of giving my virginity away at such a young age and having a baby at the age of 15. I carried the weight of other people's opinions, them looking down on me and calling my son a mistake. My son was not a mistake; he was my motivation to be better and do better. Then there was the dishonesty and infidelity in my marriage. I gave away something that belonged to my husband. I never thought I would cheat on him and neither did he.

Last but not least, trying to be this perfect person. I learned that perfect does not exist. We all make mistakes, but those mistakes are lessons; lessons that we learn from and help us grow to the next level in life. I was still this little girl hiding in a grown woman's body. I was overwhelmed by the storms I faced. Carrying the weight of my fallacies and never honestly expressing my feelings or forgiving myself for it all.

After giving a voice to what I needed to forgive myself for, I had an emotional breakdown. I was so emotional and cried for a few days. It was the kind of cry when a child hurts themselves really bad and cries so hard they can't catch their breath. That was my release. It was the breakdown I needed to experience my breakthrough. I realized I got some cuts and bruises along this journey called life, but I emerged victoriously with *powerful* testimonies—personal stories to share with other people who feel the same way as me.

My life's plan didn't go the way I thought it would but according to the plan God had for my life. It was my divine decree. I wasn't able to go away to college, but I did graduate from an HBCU. I am not a lawyer, but I went to law school and received my Master's Degree in law. I fell in love, got married, and have four children. One is not biologically mine, but I love him all the same.

No teen is prepared to be responsible for raising a child but from that experience came growth. I dealt with adult situations and had to learn how to take care of myself and my son. The infidelity in my marriage helped me realize that I was broken and needed to put God first. I needed to heal from past hurt and trauma. Ultimately, it was forgiveness that set me free. Every experience I've had has helped propel me to the next level in my life. Now I move forward in life with a mission to inspire and motivate others. To show and tell others to never be ashamed of their journey because every test they face in life is their testimony.

Regret is a word I do not use in my vocabulary. What's done is done. There is no magic or time machine to go back and fix what went wrong or change the outcome. Do I wish some situations could have been different? Of course, but everything that has happened in my life has worked for my good. I might have thought it was going to break me, but it has made me stronger. Every situation brought me closer to God. I lost my identity but found it. I found purpose in my life. My marriage is better than it's ever been. It took a lot of work to get to where I am today and forgiveness was essential.

Mental health is so important. I truly believe if we all can show compassion and inspire each other instead of judging and putting each other down, the world will be a better place. We all would be better people. You never know what the next person is thinking or going through. My story is an example of what can happen if you don't take time to heal and deal with your emotions. There is a stigma in the African American community that seeking help from a Psychiatrist, Psychologist, or Therapist is a sign of weakness. If you have an ache in your body that won't go away, what do you do? You schedule an appointment with your primary care physician to diagnose the problem and remedy it. It's no different from the stress, depression, or pain you feel in your heart. There is a medical professional out there that can help you get well. Keeping things bottled up is what makes us explode, hurt people, or even worse, hurt ourselves. I am stronger today, not because I hid behind my depression and tried to be perfect. I am stronger because I got the help I needed and put in the work to heal.

My journey may not be the same as someone else's but I felt like it needed to be shared. I have fulfilled my purpose if my story touches one person's life and let them know there is a light at the end of the tunnel and not give up hope. I want people to understand how important forgiveness is. It's not just about forgiving the person who hurt you but forgiving yourself as well. Seek help, journal, and pray. Know that no one can take better care of you than yourself. Always make yourself a priority! Mind, body, and soul.

Getting to know Jennifer Johnson

Jennifer Johnson is a native of New York and currently resides in Suffolk, Virginia, with her husband and four children. She was a teen mom with a passion for writing but put that aside to continue her education and has had a long career in the legal field. Like most women, she has been through some stuff in her life. Through her journey, she understands that there is power in sharing her experiences with others. She utilizes personal stories to complete works of fiction and published her debut novel, *All Things Come to an End*, in July 2020.

Jennifer believes that everyone's journey is not the same, but each journey offers personal and spiritual growth which is needed to achieve one's fullest potential. That is why she is passionate about creating content that inspires others. Jennifer is a true cancer who is nurturing, highly intuitive, and loves spending time with her family. You can connect with Jennifer at www.iamjenniferjohnson.com or her many social networking accounts:

Facebook: http://www.facebook.com/authorjenniferjohnson

GoodReads: https://www.goodreads.com/iamjenniferjohnson

Instagram: https://www.instagram.com/iamjenniferjohnson

A Scent of Perseverance

By

Ebony McArthur

I was born and raised in the inner city of Baltimore, in a 2-parent household. My dad who I found out was my stepdad when I was probably around seven years old after my older brother and I were playing and I got serious and didn't want to play anymore so he turned to yell 'that's why that's, not your father", he worked as a diesel mechanic and overall jack of all trades master of everything. He did not go to college, but self-educated himself on any and everything. He and my mom married when I was about two or three, so he was the only father figure I knew my entire life. To this day I have never met or had a relationship with my biological father or any of my relatives on his side of the family and no one ever spoke about him or mentioned that I ever had any other family that even existed until I was about ten years old when I found out I had a sister. I randomly received an old black and white photo of him from my mom one morning close to my 30th birthday. But I was not phased or excited about it at all, I honestly did not feel anything. In the photo, he looked to be around 19 or 20 years old, tall, slim build, and very handsome. Which were all things my grandmother and aunt had told me before. It seemed like that was the only information anyone could tell me about him, tall and handsome. I never had a yearning to know him or get to know him so even as an adult I never made any attempts to reach out. My only curiosity was if I looked like him or if we had the same smile, the same voice, or the same stubborn mannerisms, if my kids had any of his features or personality traits. I was told he is still alive so maybe those answers will come one day. My mom worked as a licensed cosmetologist, she was known in the community for doing hair and especially my hair. Her creative ability and style was well known all around the city. Even in elementary school, she would wash my hair almost every day after school to put a fresh style in for the next day. She was a teenage mom who never had the opportunity to finish and graduate from a traditional high school but worked hard to get her general education development diploma. She was and still is the go to person in our family but my mom did not play. She was the boss and had no problem owing that title. Growing up I never saw her vulnerable or loving side, she never said I love you to us, and was intentional in never showing signs of weakness. She had an extremely aggressive and dominant personality and pretty much owned the role of matriarch.

I attended Langston Hughes Elementary school in the Park Heights community of west Baltimore city. At that time when my parents first purchased our home in that community in the mid-1980s, we were among several African American two-parent families. Everyone was homeowners and working-class people and everyone looked out for one another. Everything was about community and family, kids were able to peacefully ride their bikes and skate in the streets and even if my parents were at work all of the other parents on the block would make sure we were all fed and safe. By the late eighties, everything began to change, more families were separating due to divorce or irreconcilable differences and crime and drugs started to take over our community. We owned a large lot on the corner of the block, so we seemed to get more drug traffic on our corner than the other families. It got to the point we could barely get into our front gate after school from all the people that hung on our corner to sell drugs. By the summer of my 4th grade year, my parents, after waking up one morning to brain fragments on our front porch from an overnight murder, my parents had about enough. My dad immediately called a Realtor to put our house on the market. Our property was one of the largest townhomes on the block, and we had a huge above ground swimming pool that took up most of our back yard except for a small corner that housed our playground set. My mom was a visionary and had a natural eye for interior design and décor, so our home showed like a model home and sold almost immediately.

To escape all that was going on in west Baltimore especially following the Rodney King riots, my parents made the decision to move us clear across town to the Belair Edison community of east Baltimore city. Compared to west Baltimore for us, it was like night and day. We were pretty much the only black family in this community especially as homeowners in the block of the large single-family homes. So, we faced a lot of racism. Our neighbors next door would not allow their children to come outside if we were outside riding our bikes. The local corner store owner would follow us around the store and make us sit our money on the counter instead of taking it from our hands. It was definitely going to take some adjusting, even though it was not "safe" anymore in west Baltimore, we just wanted to be around our old friends.

My mom usually worked schedules more of a self-employed contractor, so she seemed to be home a lot, much more than my dad. Not sure exactly what she was doing all day because I do not remember her ever participating at my school, being on the PTA, helping with homework, or going on field trips. She was an awesome cook though, so we always had a hot meal on the table for dinner, but her role was mainly just the disciplinarian of the house, the enforcer. Growing up I never really had examples of a nurturing, loving mom like some of my friends. My friends did not seem afraid of their mom like I did. I would hear them talk about girly things they would do with their mom and wonder why we never did things like that. I mainly leaned to my grandmother for any slither of love I ever experienced as a child. My grandmother, who is my mom's mother, also had a dominant personality so I can see where my mom got it from, but she was also loving. She always lived close to us growing up, within walking distance. Whenever and wherever we moved, she moved also, so if I came home from school and my mom wasn't home and the doors were locked, I knew I could always just walk to my grandmother's house and she would be home. I do not remember having a key to get into my own house, but I could always get into my grandmother's house. She would hide keys in secret spots just in case we ever needed to get in her place for any reason. I pretty much spent most of my weekends growing up with my grandmother, but that was fine with me, because even though our family seemed to have it all together to everyone on the outside it was a depressing, dark, mentally and physically abusive atmosphere on the inside. So, I loved the escape whenever I could get it. My grandmother would take me to church with her and sing hymnals like "Yes! Jesus loves me" to me. She would even let me come along for the super long weeks at apostolic convocation, which was just a week-long event of religious seminars and church services. We would even play games like, looking out the window of the coach bus and writing down all the different states on the license plates of cars passing by. It wasn't the most enjoyable thing to do as a kid, but I just enjoyed spending time with someone who seemed to actually liked me, someone who understood me. While my dad was always up and out of the house for work first thing in the morning and not back until late in the evening, he still managed to be more present and available than my mom. He had set up a citizen's band radio or CB in our basement, which is a mobile radio system that allowed short distance two way, person-to-person bidirectional voice transmission between individuals. Basically, it allowed us to talk to him whenever I came in from school, needed assistance with my homework, and of course for emergencies. I would call my dad on the CB radio, breaker breaker one two is what he taught us to say when we initiated each call. Even with his tremendous workload, I remember always being able to reach him.

During the mid-'80s and early '90s, my mom had grown to be extremely religious. She ended up joining my grandmother's church in east Baltimore and in line with her personality she immediately started taking charge and accepting leadership roles around the sanctuary. We pretty much went to church six days a week, sometimes seven. Between usher rehearsal, bible study, choir rehearsal, weekly devotional, and Sunday service if I was not at school, I was at church. I never played any sports or participated in after school activities with my friends because we usually had to attend something at the church. Pentecostal churches in the '80s and '90s were super strict, no nail polish; women could not wear pants, only long skirts, and modest attire, little to no makeup, and no earrings. I do not even remember having any real friends outside of my church until middle school and even then, I mainly only saw them during school hours.

At church, school, and among my family I was always known for being the smart kid. Straight "A" advanced academic, honor roll student always winning all the awards at church and Sunday school. I was the "Stop Shop & Save" academic kid of the year for most of my years in elementary school. My picture was even hung on the wall in the front of the local Stop Shop & Save supermarket in West Baltimore. I always loved to learn and was curious and questioned everything. My personality even as a young kid often seemed to clash with my mom's personality. I always felt like she did not know how to parent a kid like me. She often took my intelligence, curiosity, and love for knowledge as disrespect. It would often land me with bruises from the harsh corporal punishment and summonsing's to my room that seem like they would last the entire summer. At the time it seemed like an easy way out to not have to deal with me. I mean, I was six and seven years old getting hit across the head with broomsticks, slammed to the floor, and punched and hit relentlessly on a regular basis. I know back then "spanking" your kids was a normal gesture of punishment, but my little body just could not take it anymore. By the time I was about ten years old, I could recite most of the chapters of the bible by heart forwards and backwards because my mom would make me write certain verses 100+ times each which was a delight compared to the abuse. Maybe it was her way of getting the "devil" out of me.

My dad was not a participant of the abuse but in my eyes, he was even worse because he never stopped it either, he often stood by and never spoke up and never said a word. Oftentimes it felt like he did not condone it but just sitting back and not saying anything was just as bad. It is like he would turn a blind eye to what was really happening at my house day after day. Maybe he thought his calm demeanor would one day be the balance our family needed, it just seemed like that day would never come. It's weird because growing up I never heard my parents raise their voice at one another, or never even remember them arguing, I often thought, if his calm could overcome her storm why didn't he ever use his powers to help me? Even as an adult I don't think I could ever understand why he made the decisions to stand down, especially now that I am a mom, but I don't blame him. Now that I am a mom, I do not fault either one of them because maybe he didn't know any better or didn't know what to do to stop it, so he didn't. Maybe my mom did not have love as a child, so she did not know how to show it; maybe she was mentally and physically abused so that's what she thought a good parent did. I have no ill will against them for the decisions they made, I just knew I did not ever want to be anything like either of them when I became a parent. But I have come to a place of peace with that part of my childhood and even writing this paragraph is freeing.

Middle school was my first time making real friends and some of my best friends even today I went to middle school with. In advanced academic courses at Northeast Middle School in east Baltimore, all of the students stayed with each other every year for all of our classes, so I was able to build relationships and find another escape from being home. How our family was able to maintain such a "perfect persona" at that time I could never understand, I always wanted to reveal my home situation but everyone at school didn't seem to be going through anything similar. They all seemed happy and joyous and just fun kids so when I was at school I adapted, all I wanted to do was just fit in and be a normal kid like them. I feel like my family had mastered "having it all together" so I did not want to do anything to disrupt that façade. Middle school brought on the biggest changes in my life and those years ultimately changed my entire life, forever.

By 8th grade, I started being allowed to finally go outside and hang with some of my friends from school. Even if it was only just two or three times a month, it was the highlight of my day to be able to leave my block. My parents never allowed us to go to friends' birthday parties or do sleepovers so I was willing to take anything I could get. Most of my friends all lived in the same community which was also the same neighborhood as a boy at my middle school that I had a crush on. When my mom found out she went ballistic, she did not want me anywhere near this kid or his family. Maybe she saw something I did not as a parent, but our mother-daughter relationship was barely existent, so taking advice from her at the time was the last thing on my mind. Being only around kids at my church all my life this was different for me and middle school unmasked so many things. A large group of kids at my school were already known for being sexually active and were way more advanced in areas that I had never been exposed to. But I was not only known for being smart, I was beautiful. Unlike other kids at my middle school who were starting to go through puberty with acne scars all over their face. I had smooth brown skin with beautiful brown eyes. My parents never brought us name brand clothes but my mom was a cosmetologist so I was known for having all the best hairstyles at the school and on top of it all for a 13-year old I was built like a brick house. All the women in my family were known for having big butts and hips and the gene did not pass by me. But I never used it to my advantage because back then having a small waist and a big butt was not popular, that did not come in style until maybe my high school years. But in middle school, I remember always wearing baggy clothes to cover it up because I would often get teased for my shape by other kids and the older I got the more other females didn't want to hang with me because of it. Which was fine with me, I never needed many friends and I never really liked attention even though I was starting to get a lot of it. Due to my strict church upbringing I never realized that under all of those oversized clothes and long skirts was a body that would start to attract boys.

My parents had never talked to me about sex or boys, so I had no idea what to expect. I do not even remember talking about girl stuff like my menstrual or personal things that come with being a young lady. Nobody ever prepared me for life, I felt like I had to live and learn everything and the abuse wasn't getting any better so I was not comfortable with going to my mom to ask about anything. If I did not clean the mirrors correctly or missed something while vacuuming my bedroom floor, I was probably getting yelled at, punched or punished. I remember at the start of 8th grade on a school bus ride home some of my peers were talking about sex and someone pointed to me to asked me if I was a virgin and even though I was and had never even kissed a boy, I said no, and pretended like I wasn't just to not look like the "church" kid. I do not remember much about the day I lost my virginity. I just remember it did not last more than 5 minutes, we were kids, I didn't like it, it felt wrong and it felt like something I wasn't supposed to be doing. I tried everything I could to pretend like it never even happened. I did not tell a soul. I was so worried about my perfect reputation and the perfect reputation of my family. Yes, it was with my first crush, the kid from my middle school, he was 14 and I was 13. I regretted it so much, I never wanted to do it again. I started avoiding him at the bus stop and walking in the other directions if we passed each other in the hallways. I still kind of liked him, but I did not want him to think I wanted a round two.

Three months had past and I had never had sex again and still didn't want to, I had tried so hard to pretend like it never happened I think I even started to believe it didn't happen. Until one day after I came in from school, I was feeling like I just got hit by a train, my body was aching, I had a terrible headache and my stomach was in knots, I couldn't keep anything down. I begged for my mom to take me to the doctors, but she just insisted I should go lay down and take some antacids. But it just got worse and worse as the day went on and in the middle of the night, my dad said he could not watch me in that much pain, so he told me to get dressed so he could take me to the emergency room. My dad had never taken me to the doctors in the past so it felt like something my mom should be doing in case it was a female issue, but I was willing to go because the pain had become unbearable. After that night, my life would never be the same, the nurse walked in and revealed that I was pregnant. I never even associated the day I lost my virginity with my stomachache. I had pushed that day so far in the back of my memory, I forgot it had even happened. Thirteen years old, five minutes of life, three months ago and now I was responsible for a life.

And all I could think about was the ride back home to face my mom. I do not remember my dad saying anything to me on the ride back and even the next few days around the house no one really said a word to me. The following week my parents wanted to have a family meeting to tell everyone the news and to come up with a plan for what happens next, in my life. But I couldn't understand why my parents had decided to have a family meeting before they had a meeting with me. My parents called to inform his parents almost immediately but the days following their talk with his parents were just silent. Maybe they were just processing it all, but I needed someone to talk to and nobody was available. I felt like everyone was focused on their reputation, but nobody ever considered how I felt. I was embarrassed, I was ashamed, I was scared, I was nervous, I was anxious almost every emotion possible was running through my body and no one seemed to care. I understood that this would be hard to explain to the church and to everyone who thought something like this could never happen to "Ms. Straight A" honor roll, perfect Ebony. It is like I went from being an amazing, smart girl, always the overachiever, always doing everything perfectly, everything right, to immediately becoming the black sheep of the family. A few weeks after the meeting my mom sat me down at the kitchen table and I think her mind was already made up for me but no one as of yet had talked to me about how I was feeling about my situation. All I was hearing was how everyone else was feeling and how my situation would affect everyone else.

She sat me down to basically convince me I should get an abortion, I didn't even know what that entailed, I really didn't even know what an abortion was or what happened when someone got one, so it wasn't that it was off the table, I was 13 years old, I didn't know what having an abortion even meant. Every time I think back on that day, I feel like I may have even agreed to it if it was thoroughly explained to me but instead she used a selfish scare tactic method of having a conversation with me. She began to tell me how I would never be able to graduate high school if I kept the baby, how no one would ever want to hang with me and I would never get married or be successful. I would have another last name than my baby so no other man would ever date me, I wouldn't be able to work or ever get a successful career basically at thirteen my life was over and I was a throwaway. I never even thought about getting married at my age, so that did not really bother me. I did not really care anything about the "last name" thing she was so worried about, especially because my last name was different from everyone else's in my family anyways. She never had any talks about life with me before so maybe this was how she thought communication should be, but this method was not working. All I could think about while she was talking was all the kids at my middle school that recently got suspended, who I knew were sexually active regularly and doing way worse things that I had ever done. Some of them even had bad grades and were always at the principal's office and it did not look like their lives were ruined, it did not seem like life was over for them. They still came to school happy, playful, and full of energy as if they had their whole life ahead of them. How could I make one mistake and now it is the end for me but after hundreds of mistakes it wasn't the end for them? I was a kid that questioned everything and was curious about everything. I always looked at life from a different perspective and maybe if my mom ever got to know me, she would know that approach would not work for me. All I was thinking was there's no way I'm not going to be successful, I am an amazing person, why would no one ever want to be around me and there's no way I can't graduate high school. If that conversation never happened, maybe I would have chosen to terminate the pregnancy, but I knew all those things were not true. Maybe if she spent more time with me, she would have seen how great and how incredible I was, mistakes and all. From that moment, that exact moment, at that kitchen table, my life's mission was to prove her wrong.

So, I proceeded to move forward with the pregnancy, even if I had to do it alone. I went to every doctor's appointment alone, even though I had to catch public transportation by myself or even walk if I did not have much money. No matter the weather I never missed a prenatal appointment. Not only did my family not support me, but some people would also frequently go out of their way to purposely make sure that no one else helped me and wanted me to struggle as punishment for not discontinuing the pregnancy. If someone wanted to give me a ride to school instead of standing on the bus stop pregnant in the frigid temperatures, they would make sure it did not happen. If someone wanted to bring me things for the baby, they would make sure it did not get to me. Which was fine, when I made my decision, I was willing to do whatever it took, and I was willing to endure anything that came with the territory.

By my 8th grade graduation, I was 5 months pregnant and I felt like nobody understood what it felt like and how bad I even felt for being in this situation. I still had to put on a happy face despite all that I was going through. I could not let anyone see me down. But the truth is, I had no answers to anything, I was embarrassed, and I knew everyone was looking at me in judgment and developing their own versions of my story. All I could think was, "I feel bad for myself; I do not need anybody to feel bad for me. Imagine sitting in 8th-grade graduation everyone excited about going to high school, graduation parties, hanging with friends and here I am thirteen years old, 5 months pregnant with all eyes on me, and no plan. So, not only was I completely lost and just didn't have a clue on what my next steps were going to be, and how I wanted to move forward, I just knew that I was going to be someone special and I was going to make sure this baby would grow up to be proud to call me his mom.

So, at the age of thirteen, I embarked on my journey. I found out that it was a local school in Baltimore about fifteen miles from my house that specifically enrolled pregnant teenage girls, Lauren G. Paquin Junior-Senior High School. I scheduled an appointment with the admissions director and gathered all the documents I needed to enroll myself. You did not need a parent to enroll which was perfect for me because my parents wouldn't have assisted me with the process anyway. The school also had daycare and a health center for prenatal care on the campus, so before or after class I could attend all my prenatal appointments which was perfect because that eliminated the long bus rides downtown to Maryland General Hospital. My family had put so much negativity in my head that I was too embarrassed to be seen at a traditional high school, pregnant. The Paquin School had so much to offer but everything was not all peaches and cream there either. Everyone there had their own story and struggle; girls were fighting over being pregnant by the same person, doing drugs, and hooking school daily. But I was determined that none of that was going to distract me. I walked to The Paquin school every day, arrived on time, ready to learn. It was important to me not to fall behind on any of my coursework. I also started signing myself up to take advantage of some of the more positive things that were happening at the school. I enrolled myself in after school parenting courses, home economics, sewing and upholstery. There I learned how to bathe a baby, the proper way, how to hold and feed a baby, and emergency protocols such as how to do CPR, I learned how to make pillows, crib bedding, bibs, onesie, and tons of baby items. I also learned life skills that prepared me for my babies' arrival. I made sure I attended tutoring and additional study sessions, anything I could to make sure that I was learning as much as I could before my baby arrived.

At 5:49 am on November 11, 1997, I naturally birthed a healthy baby boy, Mhonte' Rydell. Even during labor, my mom wanted me to "feel the pain" so she would not allow my doctors to give me any pain medication or epidural anesthesia but I wasn't mad, just another mountain that I was happy to climb. That plan of hers did not work either, if anything experiencing natural birth empowered me and assured me more than ever then I could do this. I knew at that moment that nothing was more important than loving, protecting, educating, and providing for him. At that moment I became selfless, I became nurturing, I became fearless and I became a mom.

Once I had my son in November, The Paquin School, allowed students to pick up packets so you wouldn't fall behind on your assignment during postpartum, which allowed mothers to stay home with their babies while staying on track with the rest of the class. I made sure my package was always turned in on time so my grades would not be in jeopardy while I recovered. Whenever I was at the school for my postpartum appointments with my doctor, I would drop off my assignments and get new packets from my teachers. Even though I enjoyed my time at Paquin I wanted to be as "normal" as I could, I wanted to get back into a traditional high school. I wanted to get back on the path that I planned before that five-minute evening in middle school changed my life. My family thought it was best to stay at Paquin because they catered to my situation, but I was up for the challenge.

I reached out to the principal at Carver Vocational Technical High School to schedule a face to face meeting. This was a trade school in west Baltimore about an hour away from my house, that I was interested in attending before my pregnancy. They offered a rigorous business administration program where upon graduation I would receive a certificate in Business Administration that would allow me to immediately find work. On public transportation, it would take me two buses to get there but I knew finishing this program would be a huge piece of proving everyone wrong. The principal at Carver agreed to meet with me, when I arrived I was surprised to see an older white man in leadership at this inner-city school in one of the toughest communities in west Baltimore, but it was rumored that he helped a lot of other students and I was trying to be one of them. I was not use to anyone helping me so if he did not want to accept a teenage mother into his program I would have understood. To my surprise after being open and honest about my situation, he welcomed me to the school. I knew my situation would be frowned upon by other students and possibly staff and parents, but I let him know I wanted to be treated like everyone else. But I had one simple request of him during that meeting. I asked him to please keep this meeting confidential. I did not want any other students or teachers to know that I was a mom. He was 100% on board with supporting me and promised to not tell a soul, it was surreal that my family didn't even want to help me, but this stranger was willing to do whatever he could to help me graduate.

One of my Sunday school teachers who formerly owned a licensed daycare center found out about the birth of my son and reached out to me to congratulate me. During that conversation, I expressed to her how nervous I was about finding childcare for a newborn baby while I attended high school. Out of nowhere, she offered to open her childcare center to Mhonte', she had recently retired and closed her business but was willing to care for my son until his first birthday for only $100 per week. I could not believe it, this would be perfect, I trusted her and knew my son would be well taken care of in her care and that would give me a year to set a plan. The only dilemma is I would have to catch two buses to get to her, drop him off, and then walk back to the bus stop to catch two more buses to get to school. But this was the best option for my newborn baby boy, so that is what I did. During my freshman year, if my daycare called my school to say my son was colicky or an emergency came up, my principal would call me down to the office from class, escort me into his office, and whisper to me so no one else could hear, "Your daycare is on the line, you need to get to your son immediately". He would allow me to leave school and come back to get my work as long as I made up all my assignments.

During my sophomore year in health class, one of our assignments was to take home this mechanical robot baby for our reproduction assignment. The baby was able to poop, pee, cry and act like a real baby, it also had some kind of chip inside of it that would notify our teacher if we didn't feed it or just let it cry and our grade was based on how well we were able to care for this baby. Well, there was no way I was able to take care of two babies. I knew this would be the perfect opportunity to free myself and reveal I was a mom, so that is what I did. I remember everyone just staring at me in disbelief at first and their faces looked as if they had so many questions. I was tired of holding in my secret, I feel like teachers and students were starting to look at me funny anyway especially on days I just disappeared from class and reappeared later in the day for the last period and I wasn't getting suspended. I raised my hand and told the class I already had a baby and that he would be two in a few months. Needless to say, my teacher allowed me to use my own life experiences on the project and waived my need to take the robot baby home. Unlike what my mom told me, they all still wanted to be my friend, no one treated me any differently, if anything I felt like it kind of elevated their respect for me and my situation. During my time at Carver, I never attended any football games, basketball games, or did any extracurricular activities because I just did not have the time. Even though I could be a kid between 8 am and 2:30 pm, when that bell rang for dismissal, I was a mom again.

My sons dad had dropped out of high school his freshman year shortly after Mhonte' was born to help with paying for childcare and other expenses until I was able to find work, which assisted me so that I could go to school. His family was way more supportive of him than mine so he was able to get rides from family somedays and would assist me whenever he could with picking our son up from daycare when I started working. He worked a full-time job and was able to help cover a lot of our expenses for the first few months of our son's life, along with the Women Infants and Children program also known as W.I.C. That program was awesome because it assisted with baby food and formula for Mhonte'. On days that he was able to help it was a huge relief because during my freshman year I had taken a job at McDonald and it would take me three more buses to get there and back and none of my checks were more than $100 at my job but I needed every penny of it.

Attending Carver in west Baltimore allowed me to have an escape from all that I was going through on the other side of town at home. But my mom was not with anyone helping me. As if I was not juggling enough, in her eyes I was starting to get into a routine and was making it look too easy. So she started to implement a strict curfew for me, with all the buses I had to catch, to get to daycare, to school, back to daycare, to his dad's house, to work, back to his dad to pick him up and then home, it took up most of my day. I could not control if a bus was late or if my manager kept me an extra twenty minutes. But none of that mattered, trying my best did not matter. A part of me thinks she set the curfew because she did not believe that I was just at school and working. In her mind, since I had sex once, I was somewhere laid up making more babies, but it just was not true. If she ever actually communicated with me, she would have known that even though my son was almost two I still had never had sex again. She would have realized she didn't have to use these "scared straight tactics" I was already scared, and I was already straight and did everything I could to never make a mistake like that or any mistake ever again. All I was trying to do was be perfect, I wanted them to be proud of me again, I wanted them to see I was the same great person I was before. My parents never bought me diapers, formula, baby clothes or anything all I needed was a little support and that seemed like it was never going to come. I would get back home and if I was even ten minutes behind curfew my parents would have put the bolt lock on the door so I could not get in. So now it is dark, late and I have a baby on my hip and now I'm locked out. My son's dad only lived about 5 minutes away so the easy fix would be to go there until morning and leave from his house to go to school. But I knew that would only infuriate my mom if she found out which would bring on the abuse, more arguing and fighting. So, I started going to my grandma's house. At the time, my grandmother's house was probably a thirty-five-minute walk from my parent's house, but I knew that was the safest choice. So that is what I did, I knew she would let me in and not ask too many questions so we headed to her house every time my parents would lock me out after work. The even easier fix for this was if my parents just came to pick me up for work, but there was no way in hell they were willing to do that.

Oftentimes to make curfew so I would not have to take that long walk at 9 and 10 pm to my grandmothers, I wouldn't have time to stop for food or diapers so sometimes I would have his dad meet me at home while I got Mhonte' bathed and settled for bed. But my mom didn't like that either and started to tell him I was not home even though I was upstairs which would cause me to get up an hour earlier to walk to his house to pick up everything before starting our day. She would even make it hard for his dad to help me. It was already tough being young trying to figure this all out and the constant interference was becoming unbearable. If you were choosing not to support me that was fine, I was truly ok with that but deliberately making every step hard for me and jeopardizing our safety could not last for too much longer. And even when I made curfew, she would find something else that I did wrong and then back to the arguing and fighting every night. But now it was in front of my son. There was no way I could be the best mom I could be under these conditions.

I decided at 14 years old to leave my parent's house. I do not remember them forcing me to leave or even technically saying I could not come back even after locking me out they would still let me back in the next day. It was just not an environment to raise a child. I packed all our belongings into about four or five trash bags and ask for his dad to have someone pick us up. At the time I never disclosed to him exactly what was happening at my home and he never asked. I went and placed my name on the list for section 8 housing but on top of not being eighteen, other people I know were telling me that they had been on that waitlist for years. So, I did not think that was ever going to become reality but did not want to leave any stones unturned. My cousin had just rented a townhome not that far from my grandmother's house, so she let me bring our bags there, but she did not have enough room for us to stay. So for the next few weeks, we were homeless, I would put a few clean outfits for both of us and some necessities in a bag each day and we would stay between, my grandmas, his dads, and one of my close girlfriend's house that went to my high school. Her mom was so different from my mom, she was kind, loving, and nurturing but she was a little older so she never really asked questions, or wondered why her daughter's classmate from school and her baby were always at her house. Her and her mom just treated us like family. I would stop by my cousin's house every night to get more clothes and wash some of the old ones. Until all our bags started getting in the way and on one of my visits, she told me I had to take them with me. I understood that this could not go on forever but believe it or not being homeless was happier than living with my parents. But I had to put this back and forth to an end, so I went to go live with my grandmother full-time.

My grandmother lived in a small townhome and she was always taking in family members in need, so it was no room for us other than her basement. But her basement was not necessarily a living space. The only thing that was down there was plumbing and HVAC pipes, her washer and dryer, and a small half bathroom. She had taken a mattress, pillows, and a clean comforter and put in on top of some crates on the cement floor several months prior just in case my parents locked me out. So, I already had a little setup there. Staying at my grandmother's added an extra bus to our morning travels but we were safe, we were around love, we finally could have some peace. But of course, my mom was not happy about that, when she discovered my grandmother was helping me, she would pop up early in the morning before my school day to fight me. I have no idea why just leaving me alone at this point was not an option. I think it was because she was a teenage mom, and no one helped her, and it made her stronger, so she wanted the same for me. She wanted to make me independent, she wanted me to figure out life without anyone's help as she did. The only difference is she was 18 and I was 13, she was able to sign a lease and get her an apartment. She was able to work full time and get her diploma. At 13, no matter how much I worked or saved I could not sign a lease, I couldn't work more than 4 hours a day on a work permit, I couldn't even get a driver's license. I would pray every day for time to hurry up and move so I could be 18. But my grandmother always protected me. She would never let her get to me; she would just lean out her upstairs bedroom window and yell out, 'Leave this girl alone, she's trying to go to school'.

The bus stop near my grandmother's house happened to be on the same route that my dad drove to work, so he would see me outside in the rain, snow, sleet, and hail on the bus stops trying to get to school every day. By my junior year of high school, he eventually started taking a small detour of his route to pick me up and take me to school. Later, as an adult, he confessed to me that he could not keep riding past me knowing how hard I was trying without helping.

Without saying too many words to jeopardize starting any confusion back at home, he told me that he wanted me to judge him for his actions and not for anything anyone else had done to me. He did not have to say anymore, I knew what he meant. During my high school years, I never really hung out at parties or anything else as other teens were doing. If I was not at school, I was at work and if I was not at work I was with my son. He went everywhere I went, I never felt comfortable with anyone watching him or going over to family's house. I spent every available moment I had with him; it was us against the world.

By the start of my senior year of high school, it had been months since I had seen my mom but I was spending more time around my dad with our morning rides so he knew how well I was doing. Even though, I did not attend extracurricular activities at my school. I attended all the school dances and junior and senior prom. My dad was always educating me about different things so even if we had ten minutes together, he would talk to me about my plans, business, and finance. And through all the fighting and chaos, when I would see my mom, she was always stern and fussing at me about saving money for a "rainy day". So even though she assumed I was not listening through all of the yelling I wanted her to be proud of me so I started saving as much as I could. By this time, I started working at a local grocery store which was much closer to my grandmother's house than McDonald's. I could get there with only one bus, so it saved so much time between school and work for me to spend with my son. This allowed me to pick up some extra shifts early in the morning and on weekends so that by the time my son was ready to start his day I would be back home. Any penny that was not for daycare, food, or bus fare I was putting away in savings. My dad wanted to reward me by giving me a car for all the hard work he knew I was doing. So, he found a 1989 Blueish gray dodge shadow four door manual transmission, stick shift, for about $500.00 that he knew would be a perfect starter car for me. Yet again, my mom was not too happy about the reward, so the car just sat in my parent's backyard for months. My dad would always say to me 'When all of this stuff works out with your mom, you can have the car', but it was not that easy. So, I started making attempts to reach out to my mom. I think she was starting to feel bad for how things had transpired between the two of us, but again I do not think she even had all the answers on how to fix it.

One day she reached out to me and asked if I wanted to hang out with her at the mall because she loved to shop. The cashiers at all her favorite stores at Eastpoint Mall knew her on a first-name basis and when they would get their new inventory every Tuesday, they would set items aside because they knew she would be by shortly. After hours of hanging out at the mall, she sent me to get her a pretzel from the popular Aunties Annie pretzel shop in the food court. While I was in line a young man walked up to me to ask me if we could exchange numbers. I had seen him walking around the mall as we went from store to store but was not sure exactly what he was there for because I did not see him with any shopping bags. I later found out he was just stalling time while his car was being repaired at the Sears auto center. He stuck out to me because he was well dressed in a dark blue New York Yankees hat, a blue and white striped polo shirt, and blue and white sneakers that matched. We exchanged numbers that day and a few years later that young man from the mall became husband, my life partner, business partner, my best friend, and the most intricate influence on my life.

My mom and I spent a few days together here and there that month, but the relationship was just so strained it was falling on deaf ears. I think my dad wasn't looking for us to have a loving mother-daughter relationship; he just wanted peace at home, so any attempt with my mom worked for satisfying his conscious and halfway through my senior year of high school I had my own car. My dad's only demand was I could not let anyone drive it and I could not have more than one passenger at a time. Which was easy to comply with, I was pretty much a loner after school let out and being that he purchased me a manual transmission vehicle nobody my age even knew how to drive my car. Manual transmission vehicles required two hands and two feet to operate, so when my dad handed me the keys, he had removed all the mirrors on the sun visor so that I could only focus on the road. He added some nice shining hubcaps and brand-new speakers and radio to take away from the rusted paint on the exterior. I would have taken anything at that time for my son and I to get off public transportation. Having the car opened so many opportunities for me and saved me so much time. I was always big on using the 24 hours that God have given me wisely, so all the available time broadened my possibilities. I had applied to work at a credit card company called MBNA America Bank, the company was a little over an hour from my house, but I had a car and had more control over my day. I knew I didn't have to waste any time at the bus stops, when I got off an hour later, I could be back home to my son just in time for his football practice, homework or just to hang out together. I was never late or missed any of his practices or games I wanted to be there for every moment.

MBNA bank had taught me so much about credit cards, balance transfers, and interest rates, plus they paid well, especially for me to just be a senior in high school. I was making a few thousand dollars every two weeks, plus overtime and commissions. This allowed me to save so much money: I was still not worried about fashions or named brands like all of my friends. Everyone around me would take their checks and hang out at the mall, get their hair and nails done, and never talked about saving. I was the exact opposite, saving as much as I could was my only focus, so when I turned 18 my son and I could get our own place. I had already been homeless once and now living beside old pipes in my grandmother's basement, and even though I was grateful for that I never wanted to be without a solid roof over our heads ever again. My dad would take portions of my checks down to deposit them at the local credit union where my grandmother had got me a bank account before she retired from serving 35 years for the city of Baltimore. Between being a business admin major in high and working at MBNA America Bank, my knowledge of business and finance was unremarkable for a 17-year-old. June 10, 2001, I walked across the stage and graduated from Carver Vocational High School, with a certificate in Business Administration, on time with all of my peers. This was the day I was waiting to show my mom that she was wrong about me, and that I could do anything I put my mind to, but even after I attempted to reach out to her she didn't show up. It broke my heart; I had taught myself to be so strong that I never showed that any of her tactics upset me. I always just continued to press forward and stay positive. But I just knew that today of all days she would show up and show out because this is what she wanted, I did it, I graduated!!

After graduation, I immediately enrolled at Baltimore City Community College but after taking the placement test, I tested into all remedial courses. My high school was more of a trade school that focused on preparing students for the workforce. It was not a college predatory school, so I was not prepared for college courses. I found myself struggling with my grades, which I had never experienced before. I was always an "A" student. Maybe it was not being prepared as well as my busy schedule, but I refuse to give up on my education. I realized that my education was the one thing that no one can ever take from me and I loved to learn. After class one day my English professor pulled me aside to tell me he thought I was not a good fit for college and that I should look into seeking additional services because he thought I was dyslexic. Dyslexic, I had never even heard that word before and had no idea why he would say that or even what I did to give him that impression of me. But I had family members who told me I would not ever be successful so a stranger saying that to me did not faze me at all.

I continued working and attending my courses more during the day while my son was at school, which was the perfect schedule for me. Things seemed to be coming together financially but I was still in the basement. I had purchased a little blue toddler bed and a dresser to set up right beside the washer and dryer so that my son could have his own space but I was still only 17 years old so nobody would allow me to sign a lease but my birthday was just a few months away. I started reaching out to apartment complexes to schedule an appointment with the sales representative. One complex, Goodnow Hill Apartments was offering monthly rent specials for full-time college students. So, I called my dad and asked him if he would go to my appointment with me, not to cosign for me or to give money because I had plenty of that. I wanted him to be a reference of my character, tell them how responsible I am, how good I was with my credit and money, and basically, help me ask them if I could sign a lease before my 18th birthday. And as requested he did just that. My dad was well spoken and well respected in the community, so the sales rep made me a deal. She said that legally she couldn't let me sign a lease or start the setup for utilities but she had a junior one-bedroom apartment that would be available for me to move in the day after my birthday. She instructed me to come back on my birthday to sign my documents and that she would have it ready for me to move in the following day. The only catch was because I only had one credit card although my scores were over 750+ and I had never made any late payments, I didn't have a long history of credit so they required a triple security deposit equal to my first month's rent of $650.00. Two months' deposit was to be paid upfront and the third deposit would be split up into equal payments in my rent each month taking my monthly payment to $704.

My age played such a huge factor in everything thus far in my life, I felt like even if I found out someone was 16 and pregnant and I would hear them complaining it would drive me crazy. They only have two more years to be 18, that is a walk in the park. Do you know how slow 5 years goes by with a kid staring at you every day and it's nothing you can do about it? It was no way; I was passing up that offer. I posted a check on the spot for my two deposits and came back as instructed to sign the agreement to the remaining terms and one day after my 18th birthday I had the keys in hand to my own apartment, 100% in my name, no handouts, no co-signers. My dad started suggesting that I take some of the money I had saved to double up and triple up on my bills and rent. So that's what I started doing, whenever I would get large commission checks from MBNA bank I would pay my rent for three months, that would free up some of my monthly expenses and make more money available for my son and me to go to amusement parks and cover our hotel and travel expenses for his sports. As a single mom without the consistent presence of his father in his life, we started not hearing from him for months at a time. I started signing my son up for all different kinds of sports. I would make sure I took him to the best programs my money could afford. Sports helped him release his energy and taught him brotherhood but more importantly, the male coaches were role models and disciplinarians in his life. We did not have a lot of supportive family, so his teammates became family and lifelong friends of his even to this day.

Jerome, the gentleman from the mall had become a good friend of mine by this time. He had a big personality and had just departed from the United States Navy when I met him. He was from a military family so his parents sent him off to the Navy when he was only sixteen immediately following his high school graduation. We hung out a lot because he was into basketball and would play at the local park and invite my son and I to come see him play. I was initially uncomfortable with that because I did not want it to look as if we were on a date, but he never made it uncomfortable. Even when my mom did not come to my high school graduation, I looked up and Jerome was sitting in the audience. He would do things like that all the time, if he knew some important moment was happening in my day, he would just appear to support me. He was super consistent, but I was not ready for much of a commitment. I felt like he was a highly sought out eligible bachelor in Baltimore and I was a mom who stayed to myself and did not even have time to give to anyone else, so after being around each other almost every day, I decided to pull back on the friendship.

During our time at Goodnow Hill we pretty much stayed to ourselves, everywhere I went my son was with me, so everyone knew him by now. I never wanted him to feel like his mom was just a teenager; I wanted to expose him to as much as I could. I was always reading to him and giving him life lessons, and even though he was only four years old I knew he was listening. He was always respectful but full of energy. If I had a day off, I would take him for random, spontaneous day trips out of state to run around on the boardwalk at Ocean City or to get some ice cream in Atlantic City. Goodnow Hill was not in the worst neighborhood in Baltimore but it was not in the best one either, so I would drive him out to surrounding counties to play on the playground. Our playgrounds were dirty, and drug infested, and I did not want him exposed to anything like that. I protected and shielded him as much as possible from our reality.

Shortly after I moved into my apartment, his father and I decided to work on our relationship and started spending more time together as a family. We were so young with no mentors or guidance that we did not have the answer on how to be in a relationship. We tried for a few months, but we did not want the same things out of life, our goals and vision just were not aligned. On top of the fact that I was just too focused to be in a relationship. My lease was almost paid in full and I had started saving money to purchase my first home. My parents owned several commercial hair salons in Baltimore city and most of their buildings also had residential townhomes with apartments attached so I was starting to be curious about real estate. After being homeless, having a safe, secure place to live had become my only focus. I never wanted anyone to be able to put me out of my home; I never wanted my son and me to be in a situation like that ever again. I started reaching out to a local Realtor who was showing me homes and starting to walk me through the process. Things were not going well in my personal life but in business and finance, I was well beyond my savings goals. After only a few months of trying to make it work with his dad, I decided we should just go our separate ways and just try to co-parent but before we could make the split official I found out I was pregnant, again. With no motherly figures in my life, I did not know much about birth control or the effects of not taking it properly. I was on the pill at that time but had started taking them inconsistently with my busy schedule.

With the new pregnancy announcement, we agreed to hold off on the separation and he wanted to meet with my Realtor to talk about being added for us to purchase the home together. After we had the final inspections on the property, it just did not feel like buying a home together would fix our issues. Our communication was horrible, he was inconsistent in our lives and he just was not as mature and responsible as I was. Homeownership to me was a huge responsibility. I always had excellent credit and I had a few thousand dollars in the bank and that wasn't the same case for his situation, so on top of the arguing, I wasn't comfortable taking this kind of step with him. I was not nervous to buy; I just knew buying with him was not the answer. I called my Realtor and asked to be released from the contract. I was only 18 so I think she just thought I had cold feet but that was not it at all. She asked to stop by my apartment later that evening with her broker to sign the release documents and before she left, they asked to pray with us and pray for our children. I was impressed by the time and genuine concern that she showed me and a few short years later, I went on to purchase over a million dollars in real estate with her as my Realtor.

My boy's father was not too happy about a second pregnancy, we never really talked much about it. He just started to distance himself more and more, never spending time with our children or reaching out to them and basically becoming a nonfactor in our lives. But again, I made the decision to parent even if I had to do it all alone. He was always inconsistent as a father even with our first child and pretty much just stepped up to the plate whenever it was convenient for him, or if I begged him to, so I never depended on his support. Maybe he was going through his own trauma as a teenage father and not knowing exactly how to be a dad. We never really had discussions about it but even to this day, I do not have any resentment towards him. I simply preferred that he never came around again than to come around and make promises only to disappear and show up months later with more unfulfilled promises. Our sons did not deserve that. I felt like being that kind of the parent was more harmful to our sons than just being a full-time absent parent. I never knew my biological dad, so I never felt hurt or trauma from a person I never knew. Therefore, I never chased him or forced my kids to have a relationship with him, if he chose not to parent them that is a decision he must live with.

I was out one day getting some new furniture for my apartment, and as I was loading lamps into the back of my car I saw a truck ride by me, and then slowly the truck started backing up and stopped directly beside my car. When I looked up it was Jerome. It had been a little over a year since I last saw him, and a lot had transpired in my life which he quickly realized when he saw my nice round belly. But even though he saw it he did not seem fazed by it at all. He congratulated me on the pregnancy and asked me why I was getting all this furniture. I brought him up to speed and told him that I no longer lived with my grandmother and that I had my own apartment now. He again seems extremely happy for me as usual and after that brief encounter we wished each other well and both pulled off. Later, that day, he called me; my phone number was still the same as when he first met me, so I was surprised that he still had it saved on his phone.

Now that a new baby was on the way, I found myself again attending all of my prenatal appointments alone and handling the day to day morning sickness etc., all alone, but this time with a toddler on my hip. This pregnancy was hard for me; I went in and out of depression and kept it private. Hardly anyone even knew I was expecting again, I had just gotten over the hump of all the judgments and negativity from my previous pregnancy. I would often confine myself and my son to the house for months at a time. If I was not going to work, school, or sports we stayed in to just watch movies. As my stomach got bigger, I did not want to be seen in public.

With all that was going in my life, I decided that I needed a more solid career, working at the bank had taught me so much and allowed me to make a lot of money but they could just fire me any day and I would have no credentials to my name. I completed one or two more semesters at Baltimore City Community College before I registered myself for nursing school. I knew the medical field was more concrete of a career for a soon to be mother of two and I wanted something more stable. The Medix School was a two year accredited nursing school in Baltimore county, after meeting with their admissions director they granted me a scholarship to attend the school for all but $5k but I had great credit and a lot of savings so they had approved me without a cosigner for a $5K student loan. I called my mom to tell her the great news and she shot it right down. She did not think it was a good idea to take out a $5k loan and thought it was too much for me to handle. We did not spend a lot of time together so she did not know how great I was with money; my thought was once I graduated and started working; I could pay that off with ease. So just as I stepped out on faith thus far in my life, I chose to enroll in nursing school starting the following semester. Shortly after my 19th birthday, on September 30th, 2002, I gave birth to my second baby boy, Maurtice Raequan, he was born full term 5 lbs. 9 oz, at 8:39 pm. I blamed his low birth weight on my depression because I was not eating the way I should have been during the pregnancy, so I did not gain much weight, but he was such a handsome, healthy and happy baby. He was also a natural birth, my mom had put in my head that I was somehow less of a woman if I asked for pain medication during labor and I wanted to prove to her I was no less of a woman so rejected any pain meds.

Since I decided to commit myself full time to nursing school, I could no longer travel the distance and work for the bank and focus on a full-time nursing program. After releasing from the contract to purchase the house, I applied for another apartment complex that went by your income and since I was not working at the bank anymore, I did not have much income. I was completely living off my savings the past month. I was 19 years old with about $12k in the bank. My 1989 Dodge Shadow was starting to act up and I needed a new car, so I took $4k cash out of my savings to purchase a 1993 black jeep Cherokee. A few weeks later, I received a call from Madison Park North Apartments informing me that my application had been accepted. My security deposit would be $25.00, and my rent would be $2.00 a month. My ears could not believe what I was hearing. This could not be true. I knew they went by your income, but I could not believe it. The tears began to roll down my face uncontrollably; everything was falling back into place. Most people would have probably taken advantage of this program and milked it for as long as they could, but I went in the door with the mindset that this was just a steppingstone for me. If I could maintain my savings for essential expenses while completing nursing school, I would be able to graduate in just two short years and make even more money. Again, I went back to paying my car insurance for several months at a time and making sure to keep my monthly expenses low so that I could focus on school.

After the day at the furniture shop, Jerome and I started spending much more time together again. He did not seem worried at all that I had a toddler and a newborn and he loved children even though he did not have any biological kids himself. He had a stepfather that he adored who raised him to be the man that he was, so he knew how special it was to love another man's kids. He understood the importance of being a positive and consistent role model. Our relationship had blossomed from a friendship to commitment. His love for us was something I had never experienced before, he adored us. We would talk about everything, our future, my love and my interest for real estate and investments. He did not judge me because I was 19 years old with two kids; he got to know me, the real me. I explained to him what my situation was and would talk to him about my future. I assured him even though it looked kind of bad, everything I was doing was to get me to the next level and he was on board with it. I couldn't believe it, I was use to everyone around me having a motive and when I mentioned my plans to others they just found all the reasons why I couldn't make it work but Jerome was different. It is like he fit perfectly into my life. At Maurtice's first birthday party, I introduced him to my friends and family that attended for the first time publicly as my boyfriend. We had truthfully already known each other for years prior to, but this time it was different. After graduating, Magna Cum Laude from nursing school with Jerome and the boys by my side, I was ready to take on the medical field.

They always say that a man knows immediately if you're the one he wants to spend the rest of his life with and just a few months after we solidified our relationship Jerome called me from work and said he wanted to go ring shopping. I thought he was just playing but all that week he kept asking what my ring size was. I was only 20 years old, why would I know my ring size? I had never gone to the jewelry store to be fitted for a wedding ring. I never even thought about marriage, my focus was money. I wanted to be successful; marriage had never even crossed my mind. Most women dream of their wedding day but not me, I dreamed of owning my own business, having a few storefronts and rental properties, not marriage, but I was willing to go with the flow. If he brought it back up again, I was not going to shoot it down but if he did not bring it back up again, I wasn't going to either. But just like I have always known Jerome to be, he was consistent, he said when I get off of work next Tuesday, we are going to get your ring size and see what our options are. When next Tuesday came and he got off work, he called and was ready to hit the jewelry store. The jeweler tried some rings on my finger and none of them was to the standards of a ring he thought I should have, so the jeweler went to the back and brought out another ring and we both knew it was the one. But when we saw the price tag, I did not think it was possible. I would not even take $10.00 from someone before now, more less over $10k. I was an independent woman and mother, but Jerome was not intimidated by my strength, he always took pride in matching it. He knew for so long I called the shots in my life and he just wanted a piece of my heart and that was more than enough for him. We did not share this day with anyone. He only left a deposit to hold the ring that day because he still wanted to make it special and surprise me with a formal proposal, which he did just a few months later. The proposal was perfect, thoughtful, romantic, and private with just him and the boys.

Even though we were picking out rings we still lived separately, I still had my apartment and he still had his place. We would stay at each other's place every day, but we had never talked about living together. I was just coming up on my first anniversary in the medical field and continued to save. I was ready to start the process to purchase my first home, again. I told Jerome my plan and told him all about my previous encounter and the Realtor that had assisted me a few years prior. Just like with everything else he was not going to just let me embark on that journey alone, he wanted the Realtor to come by his place after work to meet with us to start the process.

I told him all about my parent properties and all the residual income they were making from their properties and he was interested in doing the same. We both had really good careers, great credit, and money in the bank, so we did not qualify for any down payment assistance programs, but we still wanted to move forward. We were excited but still incredibly nervous, we were so young and had never lived with each other before and neither one of us had shared bills and expenses with someone to this magnitude. Even though we were so young, combined we were making about $170,000 annually and we did not want to pay more than a thousand dollars a month in mortgage. I know, scared was an understatement. But at the age of 21, I purchased my first property, we purchased our first home. While we lived there, we planned our wedding and started to do DIY projects in every room. We taught ourselves how to lay tile, refinish cabinetry, plumbing, electrical, and everything we needed to know to renovate this property because we knew it was a starter home and we wanted to move following the wedding. A few months after the engagement we announced that we were expecting a baby girl. This pregnancy was kind of planned because we did plan it, but it happened just a few months before our plan. I had already had my wedding dress and booked the venue and I was worried that I wouldn't be able to fit into my wedding dress, so I wanted to push the wedding back but Jerome wasn't having it. He did not care if we had to buy a whole new dress, he was marrying me, and moving the date was not an option.

On July 28, 2007, we walked down the aisle to Stevie Wonder You & I, and before God and our family, we became husband and wife. Rewind just four weeks prior, we welcomed our baby girl Jewellz Brianna, at 2:40 am, she was 6lbs 11oz. Jerome was always patient and loving but the birth of his first biological child transitioned him into the man he is today.

By the end of that year we had successfully renovated our entire home when we discovered the house directly next door to us was under contract. We saw that it was on track to sell for $100,000.00 more than what we purchased our home for just a year ago, so we decided to immediately list our property. We were under contract less than two weeks later and profited $100,000.00 off the sale. We used those proceeds to custom build a half a million-dollar home and I was only 24 years old. This property just a few years later became our first rental property.

Shortly, after our move, we decided that we wanted to have another child. But this time it was not as easy as before. We tried for almost three years to conceive. We decided that if we weren't pregnant by the time Jewellz turned three we were going to just stop trying because it was becoming stressful and we needed to focus on the children and businesses we already had and just leave it in God's hands. At Jewellz's third birthday party, we were 4 months pregnant. On August 5th, 2010 at 8:31 am we welcomed our fourth child, Jordyn Bree, she was born 3 weeks early at 5 lbs 4 oz. Shortly after Jordyn's birth we purchased another property worth over a half of million dollars. By the age of 30 years old, I was already a landlord, I had taught myself how to effectively manage all our properties and I had owned well over a million dollars in real estate. I started to teach myself about stocks and investments and decided to go back to continue my education. In 2014, I created a custom budget and expense tracking system that helped to track every penny that was coming through our home. We were both under 35 years of age and grossing approximately $400,000 a year and counting. I started feeling like we were still investing and savings, but I also felt like we could be doing so much more. We were making a lot of money, but we were spending a lot as well. All the kids were attending some of the top private schools in Maryland, we were traveling and buying luxury cars and I wanted to tone down our lifestyle. Coming from my background I could go with little to nothing and have lived a minimalist life all my life and I wanted to go back to a more modest way of living. My expense tracking system has helped tons of people get out of debt, start a savings plan to buy a home for their kids as well as put them in the driver's seat of their lives.

In 2015, I graduated with a degree in Early Childhood Education. I know, everyone always asks how that field connects to my story. The truth is, I never wanted to be an educator in that field, the reason why I chose that degree is because I wanted to own and operate a chain of daycare centers in Baltimore. In the state of Maryland at the time, to be the director you had to have a minimum of an AA degree in early childhood education. That business plan kind of went out the door after I volunteered to watch a friend's baby for a few months to help them out. I quickly had a change of heart, that was not the residual income I had envisioned in my business plan. I wanted to go back to focusing on flip and rent or buy and hold a type of investing. That gave me the ability to make money in my sleep. That same year Jerome and I both decided to add to our portfolio as real estate investors and become licensed Realtors. That helped us eliminate the middleman; we were hiring Realtors to list and rent out our properties paying them 3-6% of each transaction, which we could easily eliminate after we obtained our license. In my first year as a Realtor, my goal was to just sell one house, with my busy school schedule, raising four kids, and managing our other properties, I was happy to just commission one property. We branded ourselves as "Mr. and Mrs. DMV Real Estate" after relocated to southern Maryland in 2015. That same year I went on to be awarded Top Producer with approximately 4 million dollars in sales transactions.

After my graduation in 2015, I went back to pursue another degree. In 2017 I graduated from The University of Maryland with my Bachelor of Science degree in Finance. I wanted to learn more about investments, stocks, bonds, business acquisitions, and financial analysts. The more I educated myself the more I began to ramp up all our retirement accounts including adding retirement accounts for each one of my children. I begin to show my kids how to trade stocks and open mutual fund accounts, Roth IRA and investments account for all of them. I started assisting them in creating Limited Liability Companies for all their businesses. That same year I launched four businesses "The Werking Mom LLC" which focuses on budgeting, savings, investments, and financial literacy, based around my custom system I developed in 2014. "TMG

Homes LLC" our official business for our fix and flip and buy and hold investment properties. I obtained my property and casualty insurance license as an independent agent to assist my clients with shopping for the best rates for home and auto insurance. All while launching my real estate team "The McArthur Group, LLC". In 2018, I graduated from the University of Maryland with my Masters in Business Administration with a concentration in financial management and I'm currently a full-time Doctorate student at The University of Maryland in pursuit of my Doctor of Business Management degree. Dr. Ebony McArthur, who would have even thought I would be saying that. My real estate group has gone on to assist hundreds of families in "Building Wealth. Through Real Estate". As well as gross over $20 million in sales transactions volume in the past 5 years. "The McArthur Group" was awarded the 2019 Diamond Club Award for overall sales volume and transaction. For the first time in my life, I am proud of me!!

If I had to give any advice to another young girl in my shoes, I would say believe in you, stay the course, and stay disciplined. One of my best assets is my ability to be disciplined, no matter what is going on around me I will never let myself down. My ability to plan, organize, strategize, and execute took me places that I could never imagine. I tried so long to be so perfect to appease everyone else and I was not at peace with myself no matter how much money I made and how much I achieved. It was all to make everyone else happy. For the first time in my life, I'm doing what makes me happy. You can educate and teach yourself to be and do anything in this world that you want to be. No matter what it is, no matter what you are facing, no matter what your situation is, you can achieve it.

Getting to know Ebony McArthur

Ebony McArthur is the founder and CEO of The McArthur Group LLC, TMG Homes LLC, and The Werking Mom LLC. Ebony is a real estate investor, financial literacy coach, independent property & casualty insurance agent, and multi-million dollar producing licensed realtor in MD, VA, DC & PA. She has over 15 years of experience in the industry and launched her real estate group in 2018. She is responsible for educating and mentoring other industry professionals on research and development, marketing, and advertising, and how to grow their business. Ebony specializes in expert negotiations, working by referral, and building relationships. She is a dominant force in the real estate industry and uses her passion to encourage and motivate others on "Building Wealth. Through Real Estate". Ebony is big on communication and takes pride in listening to her client's wants and needs to achieve the best experience possible on every transaction. She was born and raised in the inner city of Baltimore.

Ebony seeks her strength to succeed from her husband of almost 15 years, Jerome and her four amazing kids: Mhonte', Maurtice, Jewellz, and Jordyn. In her free time, she enjoys traveling, roller skating, movie night with her husband and kids and she loves to learn. She graduated from The University of Maryland with a Bachelor of Science degree in Finance, a Master's degree in Business Administration with a concentration in Financial Management, and is on track to complete her Doctorate in Business Administration in the fall of 2023. You can connect with Ebony at www.themcarthurgroup.com or her many social networking accounts:

Facebook: http://www.facebook.com/themcarthurgroup
Instagram: https://www.instagram.com/themcarthurgroup
Twitter: https://twitter.com/McArthurGroupRE

The Fragrance of A Fatherless Daughter

By

Kimberly Preston

What happens to a little girl who grows up without a father? What do you do when somebody you trust drops you?

Growing up as a child, like so many families my parents went through a divorce. A divorce is more than the end of a marriage. It is the end of dreams, expectations, family, and friendships as we know it. I remember as my dad was packing up to leave he looked at me and said, "Let's see if you will be able to get your hair done every week now" My dad was a great provider and my protector and he made sure I had everything I wanted and needed. I didn't understand his anger towards me but I was 14years old and a daddy's girl and I remember just being crushed. Although my dad was leaving I never knew that for eleven years that he would not be a part of my life. He would miss a lot of my milestones and leave me feeling fatherless. My mom would eventually shut down emotionally and a lot of the family's responsibilities became mine. I got a job at 14 years old and start working to help my mom and potentially keep up with my lifestyle that my dad told me I wouldn't have anymore because he was leaving. I remember feeling the need to always look out for myself at that moment.

I struggled with the transition and I didn't know how to process what was happening. How could my dad be a part of my life and then leave my life and act as he didn't know me? He gave me so many valuable lessons and always made sure I was ok but I begin to despise the man I once adored. Sometimes I felt I wish I never knew him because then I wouldn't have anything to compare his absence too. I became very angry and I honestly disliked him. I would call him, and he wouldn't answer my calls. We lived in the same city but I didn't know where he lived so I would write him letters and mail them to my grandmother's address, He will never respond. The more I tried the more I became angry. How could a father just turned his back on his daughter I would ask. It was too many questions for me to answer.

I had all these emotions going on within and I didn't understand how to process it all. I heard someone say prayer is a weapon but therapy is a strategy and as a 14yr old teenager I didn't have a strategy to deal with my pain. During the early '90s in my community therapy was taboo;

40

nobody ever talked about your emotions and how to cope. From dads, we learn and form beliefs about what men are how they behave and what relationships look like. We also interpret how we should be treated as women through them as well. The father-daughter relationship has a strong impact and if the relationship is broken it can cause a lot of pain.

As I was navigating through my pain I would soon meet an older guy who reminded me of my dad. He was quiet, hard-working, and a protector to me he eventually replaced the void I had in my life. My life revolved around him and I no longer focused on things a normal teenage girl should focus on. A shift happened not only in my life but in my mind: I created a new paradigm where being strong was the only choice I had. I no longer focus my energy on being fatherless but being strong and pretending I was always okay. Although my identity was disrupted, I replaced it by depending on this guy to be everything I needed. Whenever I had a problem he took care of it. He would buy me expensive gifts and he made me feel special in every way. He suddenly became my daddy. Although I didn't know it at the time I depended on him for everything. He wasn't a bad guy but he influenced me to do a lot of things that I didn't want to do. He also participated in a street lifestyle that looking back I could have been hurt or better yet even killed. He was much older than me so he had plans that weren't always in my best interest but I love the way he loved me so whatever he wanted or needed from me I made sure that it happened. I became very co-dependent on him. Codependency is characterized by a person belonging to a dysfunctional, one-sided relationship where one person relies on the other for meeting nearly all of their emotional and self-esteem needs. Over the years I learned the symptoms of codependency included low esteem, people-pleasing, poor boundaries, caretaking, control, and dysfunctional communication. Although I didn't deal with all the listed symptoms I did struggle with trying to please everyone, poor boundaries, and always being in control.

According to the U.S. Department of Justice, children from fatherless homes account for 63 percent of youth suicides, 90 percent of youth runaways, 71 percent of all high school dropouts, and 70 percent of youth in juvenile detentions. Although I was looking for validation God kept me from the statistics.

As I continued on my journey God was teaching me and molding me that my life was not my own. Jeremiah 29:11 states "For I know the plans for you, plans to prosper you and not harm you, plans to give you hope and a future. Although I thought I had my plans God always had his. The fatherhood of God can be a difficult concept for some people to comprehend given the way that fatherhood has been distorted in our society. I realized that even though my dad was absent from my life God had always been my Father and I couldn't replace that. My life could have gone another way but even through my emotional trauma; he protected me, loved me, and kept me from harm's way. Only the love of a Father could be so kind. I begin getting closer to God waking up at 5 am to pray daily. As I was getting closer to God I begin to trust God on a new level. I no longer was looking for validation through my boyfriend. I told my long-term boyfriend at the time that I decided to off to college to experience college life for a year. He was very supportive and I was happy to have his support.

In 1998 I went off to college, I chose Prairie View A & M University. Financially we didn't have the means for me to go to college. Although my dad was financially secure I still didn't have a relationship with him nor could I depend on him to help me. God begin teaching me early that he was my source. God provided and Prairie View offered me an Academic scholarship and I was blessed to leave home to begin my journey. On August 12, 1998, I would meet this country, fun-loving guy on the first day that I arrived at Prairie View. My initial plan when I met Eian was to just be friends. Our friendship quickly turned into a relationship. Eian adored me; this relationship was different than my previous relationship. I wasn't replacing my voids or looking to him to be my dad. We had fun together. Eian had been through a rough childhood and experience more trauma than I. He shared with me his love for God and the importance of forgiveness. God used Eian to help me receive the art of Forgiveness, as he shared with me his story I remember my heart feeling soft and wanting to forgive my dad. Forgiveness is the intentional and voluntary process by which a victim undergoes a change in feelings and attitude regarding an offense, and overcomes negative emotions such as resentment. Forgiveness will often be what you will need to get off the ground. As an aspect of resilience and a measure of psychological flexibility, forgiveness is best cultivated as an ongoing practice. I began to learn that I couldn't walk around disliking my dad. I had to release the hurt.

As I matured I realized that God had a bigger plan for my life. I had to make a decision and it was hard because my previous boyfriend had been a part of my life for so long but I realized my relationship with Eian was God-ordained. Eian and I made some mistakes as any young person would but we learned that God was a forgiving God. As I was navigating my new chapter in life and mastering the art of forgiveness I begin to see God continue to bless my life. In 2000 Eian and I decided to get married. I had a lot of people against me marrying Eian. I was told we were too young, we were unprepared and the list went on and on. I quickly learned that you can't always listen to people but always listen to the voice of God. I decided to ignore the naysayers and to follow God's plan for my life. I was getting married to a guy who loved God and I knew he would love me. We didn't have any plan together just our strong trust in God and belief that God had connected us for a bigger purpose. I still hadn't spoken to my father but I contacted him to let him know I was getting married and I wanted his blessings. I wanted him to walk me down the aisle, we had been disconnected for years and we never had a conversation about his absence we simply just picked up as nothing had happened. He obliged my request and on November 18, 2000, he showed up to walk me down the aisle, and after taking a few pictures he simply left. He didn't say one word or tell me he was leaving. I remember looking around at the reception and feeling that pain that I felt at 14yrs old all over again. On the most joyous occasion in my life, he disappointed me once again. I had people asking, "Where was my dad?" I did what I always did and pretended everything was ok. He had to leave, I simply replied. I didn't cry or try to figure out why he was leaving his only daughter's wedding because this time I had a strategy, I knew who I was and that God made me resilient. God had given me the heart to forgive. I also knew that I could not control my dad or understand why he did what he did. It comes a time in our lives that everyone has a choice. God had just blessed me with an amazing husband and a beautiful family and I took solitude in knowing that. I moved to Houston, Texas, and begin my life with Eian as a wife and mother. I took my role very seriously at 21-years old I was determined to be the best wife and mother. Everyone dreams of being great, there is no evil in that desire. We all want to be a part of something significant. God created us for greatness. I didn't know much about being a wife and mother but I knew that God had positioned me for my calling and I was working on becoming the best that I could. I was excited about building my future and confident that God was with me.

In 2005, I was giving birth to my second son Colin my dad drove to Houston, Texas to visit me at the hospital. He came to my house and enjoyed my family and we rekindled our relationship. I remember feeling a sense of pride, God had answered my prayers. My dad would call me periodically and then he eventually started sending me birthday cards and one day he called my phone and left me a voicemail and told me he loved me. I remember crying because I had never heard him say he loved me. I replayed the voicemail several times. I remember feeling a sense of gratitude because for years I never understood him but that was something I always wanted to hear. I didn't know that I had only five years remaining with my dad because in 2010 he died unexpectedly. The day before he died I went to visit him and bring him food by this time my dad was sick, unemployed, and needed someone. It was at that moment that I had to be there for him. Before he died I had to be supportive of someone who didn't necessarily support me. I had to be loving and understanding to someone who hadn't shown me any of those things in the past. It's one thing to say you forgive someone and not have any dealings with them but it's a different resilience to have to give and serve someone who had been so dismissive to you. I had to be the daughter I said I was and who God called me to be. It was challenging but I knew God had positioned me to show him love before he died. I was thankful for the time we had before his death but I was numb. I didn't cry I think I had cried all the tears I could cry in prior years. When my dad died I realized that God had taken me through a process of pain, rejection, and forgiveness. After my dad died I went to clean his room out and I found every letter, card, and everything I had ever sent my dad in 30 years. I believed in my heart he cared he just didn't know how to show it. I'm sure he had things he was dealing with. I want to encourage anyone to make a conscious choice to not allow your father's absence to define you and to always practice forgiveness no matter what. As I shared my journey I want to share some key steps that I discovered while dealing with my pain. Always remember Pain is an alarm that something happens and you must deal with it. Always be honest and admit your hurting. Admit it to God and one other person the impact it had on your life. Commit to Journaling on your way to recovery. Monitor your healing process and find freedom from the bondage of your pain. Pain held captivate in silence will have you explode. I'm happy that I was able to rekindle my relationship with my earthly father before he died but I'm even more thankful that God allowed me to recover from the pain. One thing I'm certain of is that God loves me. I've seen God as my Father and how he has taken care of me. You can recover from any pain of rejection, abandonment, and lead a self-directed life knowing no matter what God is your source. One of my biggest goals in life was to raise children who didn't have to recover from their childhood and God allow that to happen. On November 18, 2020, Eian and I will celebrate 20 years of marriage; we have three intelligent young men Cameron, Colin, and Carter who have been nothing but a blessing to our lives. Our boys are smart, intelligent and more importantly, being raised in a stable and loving environment. Always remember God turns pressure into power. Amazingly enough, God is so powerful that he turns the table on the tares and uses everything to make us stronger, truer, and dependent on him. I've faced many trials after dealing with my dad's absence but God has never let me down. In all things, God works for the good of those who love him.

Getting to know Kimberly Preston

Kimberly Preston a native of Fort Worth, Texas, received her formal education within the local school system and matriculated to earn a bachelor's degree in Business Management from Columbia College. Over the years Kimberly has acquired profitable skills and knowledge that were foundational to her creativity and innovative ideas. As a successful entrepreneur noted by channel Five NBC News, Kimberly was nominated and featured as an inspiring woman for her after school feeding program and providing over 20,000 meals within the community.

Kimberly has been a devoted wife for 20 years to Eian Preston and mother to three amazing boys; Cameron, Colin, and Carter Preston. In her leisure time, Kimberly travels and enjoys fine dining and prides herself on being a foodie who enjoys trying new food and places.

Kimberly believes her mission in life is to live a life of commitment to learning, living a life of integrity, and empowering others.

You can connect with Kimberly Preston through her website:

https://www.kimberlygpreston.com

A Scent of Victory

By

Erica Rose

Psalm 23 Help me to get through this marriage. How I made it out of Domestic violence, Toxic, Adultery marriage of 4 years. I got married at a young age of 21 and him 19 years old, me having a set of twins 3 years old with another one on the way which was a surprise to me and everyone that knew me, Unexpected. While feeling the need to be on my own and still living with my parents. I ended up moving to Stuttgart Germany with my parents. Once settled I ended up getting a job at AAFES as a manager to support me and the twins and the one on the way. One day I met my ex-husband now, after a couple of months of dating. He asked me to marry him and of course, I said yes, he was so excited

He suggested that we get married in Bossier City, Louisiana, his home. So we flew to Louisiana to get married. He took leave for a week. Young and in love we got married on Oct 9, 1989, in Louisiana with the help of his parents. His parents were very nice and welcome me to the family with open arms. My (real) dad and stepmom with my sisters came to support me. I was so happy to see them all. His mom help with my wedding dress getting made since I was 8 months pregnant with my middle son. Everything seems to be going well on the day of the wedding. We all were late even me because the church was lock someone forgot to call the pastor or have the doors unlock early. I honestly say I was happy to be getting married. But the sad part was I didn't love him like I thought I did I was getting nervous. I was having all the thought running through my head. It's crazy, right? I even paused saying my vows. My dad said baby girl you, okay me crying said yes. The little girl in me said no you're not. Needless I say yes... After the wedding, we had a nice reception with family and friends. Mostly his friends

My family left after the reception was over to head back to Alabama. I didn't want them to leave considering I haven't seen them in a while. I was happy to see my daddy. I'm a daddy girl. We stayed for the weekend and headed back to Germany. We had no idea how we were going to do about the living arrangement. He stayed in the barracks and I stayed with my parents (funny) until we got housing on base. It was hard for a month or two, only seeing each other on the weekend or early days off work. Once we got housing it was across the street from my parent's house. I was glad because my mom could help me with the kids. I ended up having my middle son before we got our house. It was a good pregnancy overall until the end.

45

I was bleeding out; losing a lot of blood to a point the doctors were trying to contact the doctors stateside about my first pregnancy with the twins. I'm looking at everyone's face worrying. My mom started to pray over me and within minutes the doctors came in to rush me to an emergency C-section to deliver the baby and see if they can stop the bleeding. Once in the operating room, they told my family that the bleeding had stopped. My middle son was born without any concerns, a healthy 10 pounds 13 oz. 19 inches long. The doctor said I was good and the bleeding stopped without any compilation. The power of prayer works. My mom has always been a prayer warrior for my whole family. I was released after a couple of days. I stayed a couple of days with my parents so we got the keys to the house. Once in the house, things were going well and seemed happy with no issue. Both of us are working and enjoying life. Partying on the weekend like a lot of the young couples on base.

Just being married to the kids enjoying life and everything was good. No complaints. I work on the base and see a lot of guys and people in general. Soldiers are always coming on to me. It started to be a problem especially when one of the soldiers in his unit started to flirt with me knowing I was married to you. He would come to my workplace just to say hi or bring me gifts and things. I told him I'm not able to accept anything from him. You get a lot of soldiers and spouses cheating in their military life. This soldier made it a point to tell my husband he was going to take me from him. Stop playing games my husband is like 6'3 195 he was no joke at that time. Still don't know what happened. Some words were exchanged and it wasn't good. I don't know what was said to this day. But whatever it was he accused me of cheating or leading the guy on which that never happened. I believe that when our communication broke down. I told him I never cheated on him or led this guy on; he was just trying to start drama. Shortly after this if I'm correct we were getting close to leaving (PCS) back to stateside. That's when his cousin showed up at the station at the same place. They started hanging out more in the clubs, up to no good. If I remember correctly this is when the cheating started. I knew something was wrong with his whole behavior. I decide to confront him about cheating. Like all men, he denied at first. I kept telling him that I know you cheated on me how could you do that to us in our marriage? I was so pissed I threatened to leave him and report him to the commander at his unit. If you know anything about the military the frown on adultery, he decided to come clean and tell me everything that I had already known. Call it a Woman intuition. I was so Mad and crying. We had a big fight. I ended breaking dishes, glasses whatever, I could get my hands on throwing them all at him. The house was a mess I left and went to my mom's place. To calm down I proceed to tell him I want a divorce. I didn't sign up for this Shit!

I'm a good wife to you and this is how you treat me, I blame your no-good cousin for this too. I don't want to see him ever. He's not allowed over here. After everything calmed down I went home and he cleaned up everything and apologized for cheating. I was very hesitant to believe anything he was saying to me. While all this is going on I've been having problems with my birth control. The doctor took me off of them for a week. I think that the week I got pregnant with my baby son. We all know about makeup sex. After it was confirmed I was pregnant the baby was due in February. Shortly after that, we left Germany in November for Shreveport, LA. While flying home my husband decided he wanted to stay a couple of days in New York to see his family. So once there he left me with the kids and one on the way about 7 or 8 months pregnant to travel by myself I was okay with it in a sense. I just want to get home and get settled and have this baby. I was tired and big. His parents picked me and the kids up at the airport. It was so hot. I don't remember it being that hot growing up in Alabama. I felt like I was about to pass out. His dad was so upset with him for letting me travel by myself with the kids. My husband ended up coming home in a couple of days. I was glad to see him. To be honest I was feeling this kind of way. Not happy, just miserable.

I'm praying everything works out, never been on my own. You have to grow up fast. I keep saying the Lord's Prayer in my mind just to give me strength Psalm 23.

I started to have problems with the pregnancy, not able to eat or hold anything down. I went to the E.R. at LSU medical center. I never wanted to go there. They almost killed me and didn't know what was going on. They kept telling me I could lose my baby. I can't believe it; I was crying and didn't know what to do. I could call my mom for everything. I had to just trust God. We were still staying with his parents. I decided to call my mom so she can get the twins on their way to Fort Carson, Co. until we get settled. I pray to God for healing and a miracle because I was scared for my unborn son and myself. But mostly for him, I would give up my life to give him life. Things started to get better and a month later I had a healthy baby boy 8 lbs. 6 oz. and 19 inches long. All I could do is thank God for my miracle baby. We were so happy everything turned out good. After a couple of days, we were released to go home. So it was me, my husband, my middle son, and the new baby living with his parents. It was time to move on our own. But before we move, the marriage starts to take a turn just when you think things are all good. A person goes back to his cheating ways again. So here we go again. We didn't have a car because we sold ours before we left Germany. So we have to depend on his parents for transportation. My husband would take his dad to work in the morning and pick up at night. I and the kids were home with his mom all the time helped me with the kids while hubby in the streets. I knew he was cheating or something. You know we as women sometimes are in denial hoping it is not true. Especially, since you got caught before. Now you're back to doing it again. I was unable to do anything for my family. I was trying to take care of a new baby and a 2-year-old. Once again you were confronted. This time you laugh in my face and say you are crazy. I'm just hanging with the boys. I'm looking at him like you must think I'm stupid. So that night after picking up his dad. They ended up getting in arguments about him running the street and not working or taking care of his responsible husband and dad to the kids. It was so bad I remember his dad saying he can go and I and the kids can stay. His dad took the truck. Now we screwed I'm thinking. So after a couple of weeks, I decided after we get our taxes we need to move out.

I told him I didn't care if he came or not, I was moving. I'm done with your cheating and lazy ass. I can do bad by myself. Growing up you used to hear the elder or your parents say the quote all the time. You had no idea what it meant until now.

If with everything going on I stayed with him. We moved out to our place. I ask myself WHY? Because things went to HELL. He got a good job so we got us a little car to get around until we could do better. He's always saying he's sorry for doing dirt. I'm going to do better by you I promise you. Being young and in love, we think things will change for the better but not at all it gets worse. I'm trying to be a good wife taking care of the house the kids. Making sure he's taking care of too. Wish and hoping he will change. But don't get me wrong we had some good times together. We all have ups and downs in a marriage. When growing you are taught you have to make your marriage work no matter what. Even knowing he's cheating on you. I believed he loved me. He got an even better job working at the oil company making about twenty-five dollars per hour plus overtime. I was praying that this marriage work. You think things are back to normal then you find out it's not over and over the same Shit. This time you have a female coming to your house saying they're pregnant by your husband. So what do you do? I can't risk fighting this female or I'll go to jail. I'm concern about my kids. I decide to tell him I need a break so I left and went to Colorado to see my parents and my twins. I was gone for a week to return to find out he had females in the house. He was out of control. I didn't think I let anyone know all this shit I was going through not even his parents. But they knew something was wrong. Once again his dad tried talking to him. It didn't work the fighting, beating go so bad I ended up depressed. I was mentally drained so confused about everything not knowing where to turn. Just trying to keep praying and my head-up and care for the kids. I would read the Bible every chance I got and remember watching Creflo Dollar one night talking about marriage and abuse. How we have to pray for our spouse and self but most of all you can't stay in an abusive marriage. That's not married. God wants us to be happy in our marriage. The next morning I start standing my ground with him and he didn't like it at all. They tell you supposed to be a submissive wife to your husband Old-Fashion nonsense. I refused to take this abuse anymore. I wasn't cooking for him or washing his clothes no wife duties for him. I would get hit and I would fight back the next day. He'll show up at the house with roses apologizing. So one evening I don't know what happened. It was bad the fighting I had enough of the bullshit. I'm done and leaving you to forgo. Before I could finish my sentence he pulled a gun on me, pointed at my head point-blank, and said he would kill me and the kids himself. I'm like what is wrong with you crazy. Screaming and crying ran to the bedroom to get my babies. I locked myself in the bedroom. He sat in the living talking to himself and ended up leaving. I'm so scared I had to think fast if I was going to make it out alive. I pack a bag for the kids called one of my friends I met at church to meet me around the corner. I climbed out of the window with me and my kids. Ran up the street fast hoping he would see us. I was more nervous than anything. Somehow he knew I was over her house. I told him I'm not coming home. I went home trying to figure out what to do next because I'm not staying in this marriage with this crazy man. I will end up dead.

He tried to get me to stay in no way. I refused hoping he wasn't gonna try and stop me. That was the turning point for me. I wanted to live it's not worth it. I love him but not to death do apart. I left and moved to Colorado with my parents. I was so ashamed of everything. I was overweight and depressed. Just an emotional mess adds confused too. I had a long road ahead. For a couple of months, he would call me and try to get me to come back home. The answer was No. I couldn't go back. I can honestly say I was scared as HELL. Over time he realized. I wasn't coming back. We kept in contact for the kids but the marriage was over. It was a hard fight to get back to myself. Like loving yourself to know you don't have to be treated like that by no one no matter if you are married or not. I wasn't raised like that. I had Strong family support, especially my mom being a victim of domestic violence herself when we were little kids. She understood more than anyone. My mom always encourages me to strive to do my best no matter the odds. You do right and trust in God He will do right by you. I can say it was a hard road. I encourage anyone that whatever you are going through there is a way out and you don't have to stay in these abusive marriages or relationships.

I ask that you be Encouraged by this short story of my life dealing with domestic violence. If I can, then you can get out by His Grace and Mercy.

Getting to know Erica Rose

Erica Rose is a current native of Dallas, TX moved here from Colorado Springs, Co. her hometown is Troy Alabama (Roll Tide). Erica works at Methodist as a Nurse and has been nursing for 15 years now. She loves working with people and helping. It's very rewarding for her.

In my spare time, I enjoy going to church at IBOC Inspiring Body of Christ Church. I volunteer at the church with youth and young adults with the mentoring program. I'm in the process of launching my nonprofit organization HATS in 2021 to stay tuned for more info. My activities are reading, walking, watching sports and playing sports. My passion is spending time with my grandkids in Kansas. I love my family so anytime I have time to spend with them is a blessing. I hope you are encouraged by my short story about Domestic Violence. How I survived with faith and God's mercy and grace. I learned the very storms that tried to destroy you can be turned into stepping stones to your divine purpose in life.

The Aroma of Abandonment

By

Myra Ward

We all go through something in life that makes us feel abandoned, we're not born with abandonment issues, we don't just wake up one day, and start feeling abandoned there has to be some kind of crisis in our life in order for one to feel this way. It started somewhere but where? So how does one began to feel abandoned? I can only tell you my story, and hopefully, my story will help you begin your journey to healing.

Being abandoned at a young age has a lot of side effects that carry over to adulthood. If you were given up as a child bounced around from home to home that could also make you feel unloved, unwanted, insecure, and thinking you have to be a certain type of way in order for others to accept or love you. Having a parent die before you can even get a glimpse of their face, use to their smell, or even knowing the sound of their voice, and then having someone else raise you can also make you feel a certain kind of way unless they showered you with the love that was required. Being in a bad physical / mental relationship, your partner or spouse leaves you for another woman, maybe a friend promised to always be there but somehow are no longer around, either one can bring you to start feeling abandoned.

Having had lost my biological mother at the age of one, and being brought up with a grandmother who provided the things that I needed but was never there physically, mentally, and emotionally made me feel like I had to go look for love, affection, and attention in other places besides home. Not having a father in my life made me feel like I needed the love of a man in order to feel loved not knowing I was going about it in the wrong way. Even after the loss of my mother I never remembered my father coming around not to even see if I was ok. I use to run into him as I got older but, by then I was so angry at the world that I wouldn't even speak to him I would walk right past him like I never knew who he was or that he even gave me life. I would want to ask him "how can you abandon someone who has the same blood that you have running through their veins? How could you not care about what's going on in my life? And I hated him for that. Fathers are the first ones to show you real love; they are the ones who are supposed to give you your first dance, give you away at your wedding, not just walk out of your life like you never existed.

I began to act out those feelings real early in life not listening to my grandmother, acting out in school, smoking weed, hanging with the wrong crowd, and having sticky fingers (stealing). I started hanging out with older girls wanting to be like them. I felt like I wasn't getting the attention I needed at home so I would do things that got me in trouble, and that got my grandmother's attention it might have been the wrong attention but, I still received it one way or another. I started to hang out with girls that were much older than me, and I wanted to be so much like them that I didn't care what they were doing even if I knew some of the things they were doing could lead me down a path of destruction. I wanted to dress like them, talk like them, hang out all night, do whatever they were doing. I was only fourteen they were sixteen, maybe seventeen. We would steal all of our clothes in order to match one another, we would steal cars, fight other people, and go where we wanted to go basically did whatever we wanted to do.

My grandmother would not even know where I was, who I was with or, even if she cared at all because she never came looking for me. There was a particular time I can remember being in Grand Rapids, and I can't remember what I was doing but, the girls I was with had left me there, and came back to Lansing Mi, without me, here I was fourteen didn't know anyone down there and was left all alone to figure how to get home on my own. My friends the one who I did all my dirt with, the ones I trusted more than I trusted myself would actually leave me in a place that I knew nobody how could they do that to me? I walked the streets half of the night scared, hungry, mad, and I'm sure there were other feelings I had also. The police ended up being called on me because I sat in McDonald's too long, and I was taken to the juvenile home down there, and my probation officer from Lansing had to come to get me. I was in trouble but, I was safe no longer felt scared, or abandoned. I didn't know it then but, God was with me the whole time He never left my side. I could have been raped, sex trafficking, and or even killed. Whenever I think about that time in my life I tear up because God is a protector, and He shunned me from anything evil that might have wanted to come my way. God, knew the plan that He had for my life so while I was walking half the night in the dark He kept me hidden from the dark.

The things one will do just to have friends in their life when they don't have that security blanket from home or love from the ones who claim they love you. Back then I didn't look at it the way I look at it now I just thought that was the way to get what I needed no matter what the cost, or consequence was I just wanted to be accepted, and if I had to do the things I chose to do to fit in then I was willing.

I started having sex at a young age because I thought that would be the only way for a boy to like me, or that they would see me for who I wanted them to see me as which was someone who needed love. I didn't know that my body was a treasure, didn't know that it was the temple of God, and it was for safekeeping for the man that I would one day marry. I was 18 when I had my first child matter of fact she came on my 18th birthday by a young man who I thought loved me because I had known him all my life, and he told me everything that I wanted to hear. I should have known that it was just a fairy tale because he was a drug dealer, and had other girlfriends besides myself but when you have low self-esteem combined with abandonment issues that is the last thing you see.

I really wanted this boy to love me the way that I wanted my grandmother, and my father to love me regardless of how he showed me that he didn't. He would go to jail every other month for drugs, and I would be right there excepting every collect call that he made to me hoping my grandmother would not find out, intercepting every phone bill that came to the house so that she wouldn't. I would try to please him in any way that I could no matter what he did because when he told me he loved me or that I mattered to him I believed every word that came out of his mouth without a second thought. I liked him more than he liked me, I loved him more than he loved me. I became co-dependent on him telling me I was something special to him when I knew deep down inside I didn't mean any more to him than the people he was selling the drugs to.

When he finally got locked up for dealing drugs the judge gave him about 5 years I thought I was free from being treated unworthy, from being walked all over, from being misused, cheated on, and being lied to however, I still didn't know who I was, and who was I going to blame now for the way I had been acting. I thought that maybe it was him that made me feel the way I felt I didn't realize that the damage had come from my childhood but, only got worse that's when the trust issues came about. I didn't trust any man that came into my life but, I still needed them to make me feel loved, pretty, and that I was enough even though I didn't feel like that when I was alone. It didn't take me long to find another man to come into my life that told me and did the same things that the man before him did. My second child's father lowered me in with kind words showing me his good side making me feel like I was the only girl in his life, making me feel special.

I remember sharing a class with him, and it was time to leave so he called a ride to pick us up but, before we got into the car he told me not to say anything because the girl was mute, and could not speak so she didn't like for others to talk while riding because she couldn't read our lips, and of course I didn't say anything because I thought he was telling me the truth. She dropped us off at my house said goodbye, and drove off, she didn't drive off mad but just simply pulled off. When I finally saw this girl again after about two months of our relationship I found out she could talk, and she was also pregnant not knowing at the time I was also pregnant. I left him that day and hated him for years for doing that to me. Not only did I feel abandoned but, now I had hatred inside that was growing like a tree every time I looked at myself in the mirror.

As young women or men, we just think that something is wrong with society because we don't understand "how could they not love us"? regardless of the low self-esteem we're dealing with, or the abandonment issues that we are hiding, we clearly think it's their fault when we are the ones who need the help, we are the ones needing a counselor, a mentor, someone to sit us down, and show us why we are acting out the way we are.

I walked around mad for years because of the way I had allowed others to treat me. I had to learn that others can only do what you allow them to do to you. I blamed everybody except myself for the mistakes I made in my life. Getting rid of one relationship, and then put me right back into the same one he just had a different face and a different way of using my own insecurities against me. I began to push people out of my life because of the anger I had inside when the ones I pushed away had a true love for me I just didn't know how to accept it because I was so used to the fake love, and the fake affection. I was giving more in the relationship than they were giving me so when the right people came along I didn't notice what they were giving me all I noticed was what I was giving them, and I assumed it was too much but, just enough.

It was a time in my life when I couldn't even take a compliment without me thinking they gave it with a motive behind it, or that they were trying to be funny because the compliment didn't go with how I was feeling about myself that day. I could not accept that I was beautiful inside, and out no matter what I had thought about myself. I had to figure out that if you're not sure of yourself how do you expect others to be sure of you? It was something I had to learn and grow into.

Men can smell an insecure woman from a mile away, and if you run into the wrong one they will use that opportunity to draw you in.

One day as I got older I had to realize that feeling the way I did about my grandmother, my father, and these men were not hurting them because they went on with their lives but, that it was hurting me because I was so angry inside that it affected everything and everybody that was around me. I didn't know that there was a God that loved me unconditionally and that no matter who had abandoned me in my life that He was there, and He would never abandon me. He was there before I was born, while I was in my mother's womb, and even after I did all I had done He still loved me.

I didn't like myself for years others just thought I did because of the mask that I wore. I stayed high all the time so I would not have to face who I thought I was, I didn't want others to try to figure me out. I liked being mean, it had grown up with me as I grew in stature. It's only been a few years that I have accepted who I am, and all the flaws that come with me, and even then I still struggled with the abandonment issues. I wanted to be loved, I wanted my father in my life to show me how a man is supposed to love me, I wanted my grandmother to love me the way grandparents are supposed to love their grandchildren. At the age of 16 was the first time I ever heard my grandmother tell me she loved me, and that was the only time. I knew she loved me in her own special way but, what child doesn't want to hear it, forget all the material things I would rather have felt her arms around me telling me she loved me.

Once I got saved and filled with the Holy Spirit I began to look at myself the way God looks at me. I began to love myself the way He loves me but, it took most of my life to figure that out. I walked around with a smile on my face but, was slowly dying inside with every breath I took. I didn't see who God called me to be I only seen the bad in me, I only saw the imperfections that were on the inside of me not knowing I was fearfully and wonderfully made in His image, and no matter what I thought about me God didn't see me that way. My thoughts are not His thoughts and my ways are not his ways.

As I began to read books on abandonment, anything that I could get my hands on about this subject I began to realize that the people who abandoned you most likely were abandoned themselves, and they didn't know how to make you feel wanted because they never felt wanted themselves they wore a mask just like I wore one. I realized that I was dealing with the "Orphan Spirit" that is when you feel like everyone in your life has abandoned you, and if they haven't then one day they will. I started to read more and began to educate myself and had to get familiar with this spirit, and take the head off of it because I was tired of living, and thinking the way that I was. I had to realize that losing my mother at a young age was not my fault, my father leaving was not my fault, my grandmother not showing me the love I needed was not my fault, the men in my life who left me was not my fault that was the decisions they made it had absolutely nothing to do with who I was or who I would become.

Then I turned my life over to God, and I began to soak in God's word and found out how God had an agape love for me that nobody could take away, and the things He said about me was when I finally got the picture. Now I walk with my head held high knowing I'm a daughter of a King, I no longer accept hand me downs. I expect the best because the God I serve will have it no other way. If it's not the best...it didn't come from Him. God's word started to feel every void that I had ever had. I would have a conversation with myself in the mirror every day I started making sure I told myself that I was loved, that I was somebody who was worthy of healthy love, and if I had to let some people walk away then let them walk because I was no longer going to sit in the prison of my own mind thinking I was not good enough. I refuse to be a doormat that people lay in front of the door and wipe their feet on. I had to get away from people who would help tear me down instead of helping me build myself up, those friends who actually cared I had to stop pushing away and take the constructive criticism that they were giving me without thinking they were out to harm me. I began to read on self-love, confidence, and self-worth anything I could get my hands on that would increase the love for myself. I began to write down scripture that reflects God's love for me and would say them out loud every day until they became real to me.

God is the only reason why I can stand here today, and look in the mirror knowing I love the women that I see. He has taken every insecurity and made it into a garden of flowers he has given me beauty for my ashes and has loved on me the way no man or my father could have ever loved me despite my flaws, despite what others think about me, despite who may find me attractive or not...WHO CARES! If God is for me who can be against me. I give God all the glory for how I feel about me today, and I'm thankful that I went through what I had to go through or I would not be the phenomenal woman I am.

I want every young girl, and women to begin to walk in what God has called you to be, to see you the way God sees you, and love yourself the way God loves you, and nothing else or anybody else's opinion would even matter to you. Start spending quality time with God get to know who He really is as your Father, and Savior He will blow your mind, and once you ask for forgiveness of all your sins He will remember no more. Day by day things will begin to change in your life, and He will replace every negative thing that you once thought about yourself with every positive word you could think of to fill in the gap. Every void that you have in your life get to know Jesus, and He will fill up every vacancy with an occupied note attached to it.

Start having that personal conversation with yourself reminding yourself that you are somebody and that you are worthy of being loved. Ask yourself "Who am I"? " What are the things I love about me"? What gives this person the right to be in my life?" Start reminding yourself how beautiful you are, be content with being alone if you are, stop criticizing your own self, stop belittling yourself, you might not look like a runway model however, you sure could be, and feel like one as well. Take yourself shopping get a new hairstyle do what will make you start to feel good about yourself, and forget about the naysayers because they will always be around they don't matter anyway. Forgive those people who you felt have abandoned you in your life, and start being free because forgiveness is the first step of recovery. There are so many books, seminars, counselors that can also help you with this issue, and don't let anyone tell you that you don't need those things in your life because I sure needed them and I was not ashamed it helped me in a lot of areas in my life besides abandonment. If you don't have a church home find a good one and get around some women that can help lift you up stay away from people that only want you around for their benefit than when they're done getting what they need walk away. Get people in your life that are willing to support you for a lifetime.

Loving you is the best gift that you could ever give to yourself. In order to give love, you have to have a love for yourself first.

Just remember that God will never leave you nor forsake you! And He loves you regardless of your flaws. Don't let anyone change you, and if they can't accept you for who you are they don't deserve to be in your life.

YOU ARE SOMEBODY ▢

Getting to know Myra Ward

I am a mother of 6 children whom I have raised on my own, and have done an awesome job of doing so. I am a high school graduate who went to college to become part of the Medical field however, I realized that it was not what I wanted to do. Reading, and writing was my favorite class in school, and writing poetry when I was younger just never had the confidence in me to do anything with it. I like to do things with my hands so being a part of the automotive industry has given me great pleasure. I like working with power tools taking things apart and putting them back together. I am a woman who loves God, and He is the head of my life so after he called me back into church God has put the writing task back into my heart and so this is my first journey being an Author but I'm sure it will not be my last. I have struggled a lot in my life, and have jumped many hurdles however, it was worth every jump, and I'm so thankful that I'm able to share a few with you.

The Fragrance of God's Favor

By

Krystal Hunter

Open the door! Open the door, NOW! There I sat paralyzed from fear as his hand reached for the gun in his pants. A complete and total stranger was outside of my passenger car door, yelling and screaming at me. He was calling me irate names and demanding that I open my door and let him in. Would this be the last day of my life? What do I do? I was in the middle of a phone call. I subtly dropped my cell phone on the floor so that my friend Kevin could hear everything, just in case something happened to me. Glass shattered everywhere on the passenger's side as he busted the window. He then proceeded to unlock and open the door. He grabbed all of my belongings, modeling bags, cosmetic bags, Gucci handbag, name it. He grabbed it all and ran off as fast as he could. I sat in shock and in disbelief. I did not make one movement until he was gone. "Wait…wait…Did I just get robbed? Me? But I'm alive, right? What just happened? Who was that man? Why was I his target?" Questions flooded my mind. I had just enjoyed such a lovely Sunday. The weather was so beautiful that day. Sundays in St. Louis were always the best. I enjoyed lunch at Cicero's in the Delmar Loop. Model rehearsal at the COCA building that day set in motion the tone for one of the best upcoming fashion shows of the year in St. Louis. Local designers were excited to showcase their designs and I was honored to be a part. It was a nice, relaxing Sunday in June. However at that moment, reality set in. In a split second, my life could've been taken from me. Someone would have found my dead body. The authorities would have been left in confusion searching for clues, a CSI scene. As I swung my driver's door open, I screamed, "HELP" at the first car that came my way! It didn't matter who it was. I just wanted help! I waved hysterically as I hung out of my red Chevy Cavalier! As the car approached I waved even more frantically. I looked in the car and it was my friend, Ben! God positioned him to be there to help me. God's hand was on my life. God's Favor.

Ben said "OMG, Krystal what happened"?! All I could say was," I GOT ROBBED. He went THAT way?! ".

Ben advised me to hurry and go in my apartment. He made sure I was secure and off he went to find the thief. He said he had never seen the horror in my face as he had seen that day. Ben was the type of guy who was a gentle giant. He was a very kind hearted, loving individual but he was also a protector and completely took charge of the situation.

I hurried inside my apartment crying and trying to make sense of things. I considered my area safe for the most part. I lived in the Central West End and lived on a pretty quiet college street. Most of the buildings were owned by Washington University, a top school. I felt mixed emotions of shock, fear, and confusion. I was confused that I had just been a victim of robbery yet I feared that this man would take Ben's life, yet thankful that he spared my life. I prayed with all of my heart and soul for God to calm my spirit and protect Ben's life like he had protected mine.

I waited impatiently for Ben to come back. A few minutes later, a heard a knock on my front door. There was Ben with everything that was taken from me! All of my bags! He was wounded and had even been cut in his chest! Thankfully, it was not a life threatening wound. He then called my parents. My father rushed over and we filed a police report. My good friend Kevin that I was talking to on the phone during the incident, rushed over as well. Thankfully, both Ben and I survived. God's favor.

I learned so much about the Holy Spirit that day. I remember God's angels encamping me. *Psalm 34:7 says, The angel of the LORD encamps around those who fear him, and he delivers them.*

During the entire fiasco, I was very calm. Ben explained later that he initially was going to get something to eat, but a small voice told him to come to my home. It's amazing how God speaks to us and directs us.

A few weeks later, I ran into a model buddy, Pierre. Pierre lived right around the corner from where I had been robbed. He asked where I had been. I explained the incident that occurred and he began to ask me questions about the guy. "What did he look like?" "Describe him", said Pierre.

As I described his cornrows, glassy eyes, white t-shirt, and jeans, he looked in amazement. He said," I know that guy. That was Kraig J! Kraig was arrested for attempted robbery of the bank last week!"

I couldn't believe that God was revealing the full name of the man who robbed me! God's favor. I took the information and provided it to the police department.

That incident was one of the most horrifying incidents that I have been through, yet it was the catalyst for my spiritual growth. Jehovah God gave me the strength and the perseverance to continue my life's journey. I knew that Satan wanted me to stay paralyzed in fear. I knew that Satan was trying to rob me of my life and was also in pursuit of my mind and soul. I just continued to reflect on the fact that God had plans for me. *Jeremiah 29:11 says, For I know the plans I have for you," declares the LORD, "plans to prosper you and not to harm you, plans to give you hope and a future.* I used my faith in God to bounce back. I decided to move to Atlanta,

Georgia. I wanted a fresh start and new environment. I left on a Friday night with $300, a bag full of clothes, and my faith for a new beginning. I let the incident go, so I thought.

As I arrived, one of best friends, Aaron, made sure that I had home accommodations. He also informed me about a job fair at a Telecommunications company. I went the day after I arrived in ATL. I was hired on the spot and started work on Monday! That was the great thing about Atlanta, endless opportunities everywhere. I worked there for a few months, was a top sales representative, and received an amazing opportunity as a Loan Officer with a top mortgage company. Just weeks later, I was enjoying the cool breeze of Georgia, eating in Buckhead at top of the line restaurants sponsored by my company. I tripled my salary. They even flew me to Ft. Lauderdale for paid training in an all-inclusive in a resort style hotel on the beach. God's Favor. Surely, God had a plan for me. Just weeks prior I had been through one of the worst experiences of life, yet God was presenting to me with new opportunities, amazing experiences, and new connections!

Although things were going great, there were days that I felt depressed. I was booked for modeling jobs. I was hired by Mercedes Benz as ambassador, Vibe Vixen wanted me to model for them in Los Angeles. I even had a German designer interested in me touring with him. I enjoyed VIP at exclusive events. Everything was happening so fast. I would network and hear how beautiful I was, yet I felt so much pain inside. Beauty didn't bring happiness. I was in an emotional fight. Counterfeit men would come my way, pursuing and running game left and right. There was an employee trying to set me up on my job. There was also an employee that was very suggestive and would say sexually inappropriate things to me. In addition, a man that I dated and was no longer interested in began to stalk me at my job, call into my office, and leave me insane voice messages at home. I was on an up and down emotional roller coaster. I was ballin' as they say, but I still didn't completely have the peace I longed for. Things had come back together just to fall apart.

I couldn't understand if I had survived that incident back home in St. Louis and God was providing me with so many "suddenly" blessings, why was I so unsettled in my spirit? Out of the blue, amazing things would happen yet there was still an emptiness inside. Well, the more I began to pray, spiritual aha moments began to happen. God revealed to me that was suffering from trauma and running from my pain. I could no longer run from things that were impacting my emotions and spirit. My moral compass became more sensitive. God reminded me that he preserved my life for a reason. That no weapon formed would prosper. *Isaiah 54:17 says, No weapon formed against you shall prosper, and you will refute every tongue that accuses you. This is the heritage of the servants of the LORD, and their vindication is from Me," declares the LORD.* God made it very clear to me that he would always be protector and my safe place. That no relationship, no job, no matter how much money I made, nor beauty would give me PEACE. I opened up my heart to Him and gave him the steering wheel of my life. Building my relationship with him was a true game changer.

That's when the healing began. My discernment grew stronger. Once I began to walk in my power, I no longer felt that I was a victim of circumstance. I claimed the title front- line warrior, a Lioness, and claimed the victory as mine!!! I spoke life to myself daily. "I am the head and not the tail. I am above and not beneath. I have God's favor. I have purpose. God wants to use me to change the world, spread his message, and encourage others that they can do all things by Christ who strengthens them! (Philippians 4:13 says, I can do all things through Christ who strengthens me.). There was no longer a need to numb my pain. I had a natural healer directing my course. I experienced True Freedom, Resilience, Strength, and Confidence.

20 years later, I still maintain a very intimate relationship with my Father, Jehovah God. Throughout the years, I've had my share of ups and downs, however I've matured so much spiritually. God has rescued me and favored me in situations that you would not believe! I am grateful that my parents gave me a solid spiritual foundation as a child (Proverbs 22:6 says, Train up a child in the way he should go, And when he is old he will not depart from it) They still encourage me and I am so grateful for them. I've been able to pass on these gems to my daughter, Kailey. As I have matured, I can truly see the benefit of having a spiritual family and how staying close to Jehovah can help you navigate life and stay safe in his hedge of protection when the enemy strikes. His love is a love like no other.

My ultimate goal is to not just share my experience of triumph with the world. I am here to encourage you and remind you of who you belong to. You are a child of God. It doesn't matter what life throws at you. You have the ability to overcome adversity. You may ask how? How do I get the peace and maintain the peace? How do I overcome the obstacles that come before me?

The first thing you must do is Forgive. Releasing the anger that you have for yourself and others, allows your heart to be cleansed, free for God to enter in. Forgiving the man the robbed me was a challenge but in the process I developed compassion for him. What a sad, broken, and desperate soul to make such a drastic decision that night. What was his life like? Clearly a sad one. *Luke 23:34 says "Father, forgive them, for they know not what they do."* Release and allow God to heal your trauma. He is a just God and will give you peace in the situation. I continue to practice forgiveness for those that have hurt me and ask God for forgiveness, since I am also imperfect.

Secondly, Believe. You have to believe with every fiber of your being that Jehovah has plans for you. You must walk in expectation of what God can do for your life. Once you believe it, SPEAK IT! Every morning and night speak daily affirmations. Read the word and fill your spirit daily. Know that it's on its way, no matter HOW things look. Keep your eyes yet not on the situation, but on HIM. Know that your Father will take care of you. *Proverbs 18:21 says, Life and Death are in the power of the tongue, and those who love it will eat its fruit.* If you have a negative mouth, you will most likely produce a negative life.

After you truly believe that God has a plan for you, write the vision and make it plain. *Habakkuk2:2 says The LORD answered me: Write down this vision; clearly inscribe it on tablets so one may easily read it. List your dreams, goals and pray over your list. Don't obsess over it either.* After you've made your petitions known to God, let it go. Release the steering wheel to Him. Release the attachment to the desire. Obsessive attachment creates fear. He will work it out on your behalf. When things don't work out as planned, it's only because God has greater for you. It is important to keep your vision in front of you in expectation of great things, God's Will. He is always behind the scenes orchestrating. When you Trust the process. Know that what He has for you is on the way and bigger than you can imagine! He works on his timing. He loves you so much and wants you to have His best! Wait on him. His vision is even bigger than yours. Don't settle.

Lastly, once you believe and write your vision, pray over your list and take immediate action! What steps can you take to create the life that you want? You are not your past nor your trauma or experiences. When you are excited about your life, you won't get stuck in the past. You will be able to be resilient and get excited about your future! As a matter of fact, you will begin to thank God for those painful experiences. God is always doing a new thing, so you have a lot to look forward to! Let's Go! *Isaiah 42:18-19 says, Forget the former things; do not dwell on the past. See, I am doing a new thing! Now it springs up; do you not perceive it? I am making a way in the wilderness and streams in the wasteland.* You will be grateful and proud of yourself for being a conqueror and overcoming your trials and tribulations. When you make a decision to be free, God will help you walk into freedom and remain free. *Romans 8:28 says, And we know that in all things God works for the good of those who love him, who have been called according to his purpose.* Surround yourself with a support system of people who pour into you. A circle of safety is necessary for your growth. If you don't have anyone that you feel is a positive, pray over the matter and God will send you the right people at the right time. Use that time of being alone to grow and prepare for what's to come.

Ben was an amazing friend that put his life on the line for me! We are still friends of over 20 years. He is one of my closest friends and I am eternally grateful for him. I've also know Kevin for over 20 years. He had my back and supported me on the scene of the crime. It is truly appreciated. My friend Aaron in Atlanta helped me get set up. I am blessed with so many amazing friends and family members. I thank God for all of them. I am grateful for my kindred brother Chris for reinforcing God's Favor on my life hence, such an amazing title for my chapter.

What is your personal struggle? Fear, Anxiety, Depression, Loneliness, Frustration, Shame, Breakup, Divorce, Finances, Illness, Death… Do you constantly find yourself asking, "When God"? "Why God"?

He will answer.

You may have a laundry list of circumstances that you are battling. I'm sure many can agree that 2020 has been a challenging year for many. So many have suffered from loss on multiple levels. Did you know that even in a pandemic, God can make your dreams come true? Yes, even in a pandemic. Throughout history many millionaires have been born during a pandemic. The Covid-19 pandemic is no different.

I've had awesome things happen to me this year out of the blue, including writing this book! Many have used job loss as an opportunity to be entrepreneurs. Pandemics create Millionaires. The quarantine has also opened up the eyes to so many in relationships which has resulted in many engagements and marriages have taken place! People are now seeing what matters most. So always trust God. He is a "Suddenly God" and can make it happen in an instant, no matter what things look like! Just. Like. That! There is always purpose in pain. The enemy attacked me with bronchitis and a car accident at the final stages of completing my submission for this book. But guess what? Here it is. Nothing can stop what God has for us.

If you're feeling alone, lean on Him. He knows. He cares. He will bring beauty to ashes. *Isaiah 61:3 says, To all who mourn in Israel, he will give a crown of beauty for ashes, a joyous blessing instead of mourning, festive praise instead of despair. In their righteousness, they will be like great oaks that the LORD has planted for his own glory.* Don't be ashamed or live in guilt. God wants to free you and can free you.

You are winning! Make a promise to yourself and most importantly to God, that you will take steps to be delivered starting today. Allow yourself the time and grace to be free. In the words of Donnie McClurkin," We fall down but we get up"! It's time to stand up and take back everything the enemy stole from you. God will make it happen. He tried to rob me of my destiny, my mind, my heart, and even my belongings, and even my life! But guess what? God gave it all back to me and I'm better than ever. He cannot have what is rightfully yours. Don't give up. Speak with Authority and Join me in this freedom journey. My friend know that You are delivered! You are resilient! Speak it every day until it manifests! I am praying for you. You are resilient, amazing, and can have The Fragrance of God's favor on your life if you want it! Trust God, Protect your spirit, Know that All is Well…and it is so, in Jesus' name, Amen.

With Love,

Krystal Hunter

Getting to know Krystal Hunter

Krystal Hunter is a loving Empowerment Coach, Author, and Mentor to women and girls. Her warm and down to earth approach to life and others, is the reason why so many love her message. Krystal believes that her relationship with Jehovah has allowed her to be used as a vessel to others, and fulfill her calling. In addition, Krystal is multi-talented and wears many hats. She was born a Fashionista. As a former fashion model, she decided to open a business called Beautiful Swag that encompasses "all things beauty". She embraces the Information Technology World as a Certified Scrum Master. In addition, She is a Massage Therapist and loves the healing arts. Krystal's ultimate goal is to use all of her gifts to empower women and girls to prosper and manifest everything God has for them. Krystal is the proud mother of a vibrant, creative 14 year old violinist, Kailey. They reside in Frisco, Texas.

The Sweet Savor of Rescue & Recovery

By

Shelva Cox

It has always been in the ultimate plan of God to one day not only redeem His creation but also fully restore us back to our original state; the state in which He created all mankind, in His image and His likeness. Jeremiah 29 and 11 simply remind us that even before we were formed-(bring together parts or combine to create something) in our mother's womb, God knew us. In other words, before you were ever a twinkle in your daddy's eyes or even a thought in your mother's mind, God had already established a relationship with you in eternity. Here the word "knew" is the past tense of "to know" which in Greek it is pronounced Ginosko-meaning intimacy or relationship. So, we are reminded in Genesis 1 & 27 that before mankind was formed out of the dust of the earth, we are created spiritual beings in the image and the likeness of our Creator. Therefore, our first and sole purpose in life is to have a relationship with our Creator. This lets us know that God truly has the perfect plan and destiny all mapped out for our lives, for whom He foreknew (knew before in eternity) He also did predestinate. Therefore, being in constant fellowship with our creator, He will in return reveal our destiny in life.

Growing up and being reared in the church, my grandfather-the late Bishop Alex Wall and my grandmother-the late Mother Leddie Marie Wall made sure that I was trained up in the ways of God. My grandfather not only provided great biblical teachings but he also baptized me at a very young age. I remember every Saturday morning during service; the whole congregation would read The Ten Commandments. I didn't understand then but I know now that it was God's way of engrafting His word of laws and statutes down off inside of me for His divine purpose in my life's future posterity.

Growing into adolescence is when things shifted and I began to experience activity that no 9-year-old should ever have to go through. This traumatic occurrence did more damage mentally and psychologically than the actual bodily harm. This type of damage left an embedded hollow space of darkness that lingered with my soul or psyche-which comprises the mental abilities of a living being. Therefore, this affected my reason, character, feeling, consciousness, memory, perception, thinking, etc. Trauma causes you to get "stuck" in an abnormal state in which development has prematurely stopped. This is known as Arrested Psychological Development. Yes, the traumatic occurrence I'm talking about is sexual abuse. In my situation, it was not the abuse by the hands of a man, it was the total opposite. I was sexually misused from gentle strokes and soft caresses by another female. This particular teenager was in high school and yes a very close friend of our family but I was only an innocent child. How did I know this type of sexual contact was wrong? However, like the majority of children do, I never told anyone or shared my experience. I simply suppressed those very acts and stored them away back of my mind. Honestly, I never thought about it again. Oh, but the magnitude of damage was festering…. only God knew.

Even as a young girl, I remembered always feeling so unhappy for no apparent reason. My mom uses to tell me that pleasing me was nearly impossible. Nothing she did ever seemed good enough to me anyway. Yes, I was her problem child! And my cousins would tease me and say that my lips looked like a "duck's booty" because they stayed poked out so much. Apart from being mad I just used to feel so unhappy and also during that time when I started urinating on myself during nights while sleeping. One particular morning, after my grandmother woke us up for breakfast, I heard her changing the linens and immediately knew that I was in trouble. She discovered that I had indeed wet the bed… again. For her, washing sheets had become a daily ritual and well, I guess this time was "the straw that broke the camel's back". Grandmama was fed up!! Missy (my nickname) and got the worst whooping ever. I guess she figured out if she gave me the rod of correction I would stop urinating in her bed. It was truly the worst whooping I'd ever received from my grandmother. Did y'all ever get those kinds of whooping's that made you wet yourself while you were in the very act of getting the whooping? Yeah, that was this kind. We didn't receive spankings, we got whooping's growing up. Even back then; I still didn't understand what was causing me, at ten years of age, to have that issue but neither did my grandmother. At least I did not think she knew because I don't remember her ever asking me if anything was wrong. However; now I understand that it had to do with the sexual trauma. If you recognize sudden changes in your child's behavior and they have started acting out in more ways than one…talk to them. Most kids don't tell. They find other outlets to release that bottled up frustration.

So for several years after that, I struggled with not only having low self-esteem, I practically lived in a state of depression. I even came to the point of deciding that life was just not worth living anymore so I attempted suicide. I remember getting up one day, looking in the mirror, and just hating myself. One by one I consumed a total of twenty pills then laid in my bed and drifted off to sleep. I'm not sure how long I slept but I eventually woke up after feeling a slight little nudge. At that point, I became very afraid after realizing those pills were still inside me. I called the emergency room then I called my mom. When I finally made it to the hospital, I was given some type of black liquid to drink which caused me to throw up everything that I had consumed that day. I remember my mom-Jeannie Sue briefly coming and sitting on the bed, reassuring me of just how much she loved me. After a while, she left and headed back to work. Then my bonus dad-Donald Ray came in and sat with me for the remainder of my hospital stay.

Even after that, my life became full of more issues and more drama. I not only became very promiscuous but all the guys I had relationships with, were always younger than I was. Although I was aging and growing physically, my emotions were still held captive from the trauma and so I seemingly gravitated towards dating guys who were younger than me. Simply because that was the emotional level I was "stuck" at. However, I did eventually make my way to college, moved into a dorm, and even pledged to a sorority social club. Everything was going great and I was digging the college vibe life. There were dances every weekend and sometimes partying until the wee hours of the night. I felt footloose and fancy-free. Well, shortly thereafter, I became involved with a young man on campus and fell head over heels in love. He was the most gorgeous looking guy that I had ever laid eyes on. Many of the young ladies on campus were just as smitten over him as I was but he found an interest in this small town country girl. He was tall with a high yellow complexion with jet black curly hair and the cutest little freckles all over his face. He was so gorgeous to me and I just knew one day I would marry him. However; it didn't last very long and shortly thereafter; we had gotten into a big altercation and he broke up with me. My heart was crushed and I was devastated! I just couldn't handle the rejection and so once again, I found myself right back in that state of depression. So yes I attempted to end my life for the second time. The cycle seemed to have repeated itself and the spirit of suicide had once again found my location. I ended right back up in another emergency room but this time with a tube down my throat. They pumped those pills out of my stomach. And as I laid there on the hospital bed, tears streaming down my face, arms strapped to the bed so I wouldn't pull the tube out…..all I could do was think about the fact that if these pills don't take me out, surely this machine was going to kill me. I had never experienced anything like that in my life!!! So after all was said and done, and much evaluation by the counselor on campus, I was advised to withdraw from my classes and go home. My mom and "bonus dad" then drove 10 hours from West TX to East TX and picked me up! Even after that, I became like a ticking time bomb…popping off on whoever, whenever. I stayed in quarrels and altercations. If I thought you looked at me wrong, it was a problem!! I did not care!! All that anger was bottled inside and I still had no idea why!

Well, in the midst of all that, some years later, I found myself in the role of a single mom, raising two children by different men. I remember being several weeks pregnant with my second daughter and found myself in an abortion clinic. After examination by the doctor, I was told that I was two weeks too far along and would not be able to abort my unborn baby because the fetus was too big for him to carry this procedure out. If you are reading this and you have found yourself in this situation, I want to encourage you and let you know it's okay. You are going to make it. Your child will be a blessing to you no matter how he or she was conceived. God says that the baby is not a mistake and you are not a failure! You are loved and your baby will bring you so much joy!! Hang in there because your life matters. God still loves you and cares so very much about you! He has a master plan. I speak encouragement into your spirit…. you're going to make it!! Well after returning home that day, I found myself sitting on the bed sobbing uncontrollably. So many negative thoughts beganto fill my mind…thoughts of me not ever being wanted or loved by a man again. I remember feeling so worthless, so unloved, and in such a state of hopelessness. Even as I sat there waddling in my situation; I suddenly heard a voice say "IT'S NOT WHO YOU THINK IT IS" and I knew exactly what that voice was talking about. I immediately stopped crying and begin looking around the room because there was no one else in my apartment but me and my one and a half-year-old daughter. Simply hearing that voice brought peace to my mind.

However, that still didn't negate the fact that I had no clue about parenting. I found myself always yelling and spanking them for no apparent reason, mainly because I had no patience and always felt frustrated by the cares of life. I still hadn't dealt with my anger issues nor had I even ever acknowledged it as being an issue. Remember you can never conquer something if you never identify it.

And so, day by day struggles from being a single mom became overwhelming at times. I couldn't seem to ever keep a job and therefore; I had no other choice but to live off government assistance. I never had any support from the biological dads because they both chose not to be a part or active in my children's lives. If the truth is told, I neglected some of my parental responsibilities as well by choosing to go out clubbing, smoking, and drinking. So yes, there I was, a 23 years old mother old with no sense of direction in life what-so-ever. I didn't have any goals, aspirations, or dreams of becoming anything or anybody in life, no desire to return to college, and continue my education further…nothing! My focus and priorities were all misconstrued and I merely existed, day in and day out! Although I had been reared in the church, not one time did I ever consider surrendering my life to God. Not one time!

Until one day…..I found myself kneeling on my oldest daughter's bed …just weeping …it felt like I was carrying the weight of the whole world on my shoulders and I just couldn't take it anymore. Has anyone ever felt like this? Can I get a witness? So much hurt, so many disappointments, so much guilt, so much shame, and so much anger. I didn't say a word but at that moment I simply thought to myself "Lord I cannot take this" and I begin to weep even louder and cry even harder … But it wasn't until I cried out and said "JESUS PLEASE HELP ME" …and when I tell you without hesitation or questions asked, there came a supernatural force that I had never felt before in my life. Immediately I could feel that weight being lifted from off of me. Hallelujah!! In my distress, I cried unto the LORD, and he heard me (Psalms 120:1) Wherever you are that's where Jesus will meet you and He will help you. He is ready to rescue you! That day was indeed a pivotal moment in my life. After I surrendered and asked Jesus to come into my heart from that day forward my way became so much clearer. If you have been doing things all by yourself and it's still not working, I encourage you to call on Jesus. He is waiting right where you are to help you in only a way that He knows how! You have tried every physician; you have tried every psychologist. You have even sought out the best your money can buy. But I'm here to let somebody know that Jesus is the key to your breakthrough! Surrendering my life and asking Jesus to be my Lord and Savior was the best choice in life I have ever made. It was a done deal! And not only did he rescue me he redeemed me back to Himself. I know that I am bought with the price. That price of God's amazing grace. I'm talking about the cross at Calvery because I know Jesus shed His blood not just for me but for you too. And see that is the key to this faith walk. Hebrews 11:6 states that But without faith it is impossible to please Him, for he who comes to God must believe that He is (He is real and He does exist) and that He is a rewarder of those who diligently seek Him. I experienced something that I never felt in my entire life before…and that is the peace of God that transcends all understanding. It was such a calmness that came over me. And right now I speak that same peace in your mind and your spirit! I just knew beyond a shadow of a doubt that Jesus was with me. And even the days that He seemed so far away my faith assured me that He was right there by my side! And so yes that very day I proclaimed Romans 10:9 & 10: That if thou shalt confess with thy mouth the Lord Jesus, and shalt believe in thine heart that God hath raised him from the dead, thou shalt be saved. For with the heart, man believeth unto righteousness; and with the mouth, confession is made unto salvation …That was a special day because I chose Him to come to live down on the inside of my heart and He became my everything!! For in him I live, and move, and have my being; Acts 17:28. So as His child, He took me by the hand and whispered "I will never leave thee, nor forsake thee." (Hebrews 13:5) He begins to walk and talk with me daily…and in a still small quiet voice, he begins expressing His love and adoration for me and all of His creation. He became my first love, my Ish-my husband. And ladies this is key, in Proverbs 18;22, have you ever wondered why that scripture says "He that findeth a WIFE….well by definition of a wife it means a married woman considered about her spouse. God is merely calling you His wife…. Selah! That's right; He wants you to be in an exclusive relationship with Him FIRST! No, if and's or buts about it! He wants to be the center of your joy and He wants your undivided attention. He wants more than just a one-night stand! He wants all of you! He wants you to be dependent on Him. Whatever you need, He said to ask Him! I begin to know Him as my provider and the one who made ways out of no ways. It was just Him and I … we were a couple! He said, "Shelva, whatever you need me to be I AM THAT I AM" When I tell you the sweet nothings that He would whisper in my ear….. He is a total gentleman! He set the bar for anyone coming after! That is why you must not settle. God is preparing you and making you ready for your Ephesians 5:25 husband that will love his wife even as Christ also loved the church, and gave himself for it; DO NOT SETTLE! God said I will supply all your needs according to my riches in glory (Philippians 4:19). At this point, He then begins teaching me how to be a nurturer for my children. As I found myself spending more and more time with Jesus, I began 'to know' (as in the Hebrew word Yada-acquaintance; to be learned, understood, and having understanding) Him for myself. And although I was reared in the church, we all know that relationships hit different when they are personal. I found myself reading the bible quite often, meditating on His word day and night, praying more, and even going to church regularly. His word reminds us that blessed are those who hunger and thirst for righteousness, for they shall be filled" (Matthew 5:6). If you've come this far reading and you feel emptiness or a void inside of you, then I decree right now IN THE MIGHTY NAME OF JESUS that He is filling that void. By faith, it shall be done. He then began to show me, by way of scriptures, just how much He loved mankind (read John 3:16) Oh' He loves you so much!! And He cares about every area of your life. He truly desires you to be healed and set free. He said "Shelva your value to me is far greater than rubies, diamonds, and any hidden treasure" He showed me my self-worth! And for me to always remember there is no condemnation to them that are in Christ Jesus, who walks not after the flesh but after the Spirit (Rom 8:1). Grace says you don't have to carry the guilt or the shame. Just accept the "sufficiency of Grace" provided and keep it moving. I am my Father's child. Even while continuing on this spiritual journey, He began to walk me back to my childhood and uproot that root of bitterness (Hebrews 12:14-16) that had been planted from my childhood. That's where all that anger stemmed from. So just imagine the roots on a big Oak Tree and how they grow down in the dirt…..all those years and how that root of bitterness took root and grew in my soul from the sexual trauma!! BUT GOD!! He then delivered me from all that hurt, all the shame of my past, all those soul ties from being promiscuous….and He healed that wounded little girl. That's why we must always allow life's trials and tribulations to push us in the direction toward Jesus! He is our Father and the one who helped me to forgive my abuser. Understand that forgiveness is a way of releasing ourselves from the pain we experienced at the hands of others. Forgiveness is not for the perpetrator, it's for you! I was never given the opportunity to talk to a psychiatrist but what I did do was fall on my knees and pour my heart out to the one I knew could restore me. Whom the Son sets you free, you will be free indeed (John 8:36) Jesus was the only one who knew more about me than I knew about myself. He performed spiritual surgery and gave my identity back! Oh' and this beautiful smile that I wear so well, He painted it on my face. He said no Father wants to see their daughter unhappy. And so after doing all that, He then declared "And You Shall Recover All" (I Samuel 30:8) Yes, everything that the enemy stole…your joy, your dignity, your sanity, and even your identity. RIGHT NOW I DECREE ISAIAH 61:7 OVER YOUR LIFE, THAT WHATEVER THE ENEMY HAS STOLEN FROM YOU, I DECREE THAT YOU SHALL RECEIVE DOUBLE FOR YOUR TROUBLE.

It's only by God's grace that I am the resilient woman I am today. God said, "Your greatest set back was merely a set up for your come back!" I know who I am and to whom I belong! As a child, I didn't understand a lot of things but after I gained wisdom, knowledge, and understanding concerning spiritual warfare, I recognized my abuse was an attack launched from the kingdom of darkness to try and thwart God's plan and purpose for my life. For we do not wrestle against flesh and blood, but principalities, against powers, against the rulers of the darkness of this age, against spiritual hosts of wickedness in the heavenly places. (Ephesians 6:12)

The devil used that young lady to rob my innocence and caused me to have an identity crisis. That devil tried to literally 'turn me out" but what the enemy meant for evil against me, God has turned it and now uses it for good(Genesis 50 & 20) That's why I can now unashamedly and boldly tell my story and share how God rescued me. Who did it? God did! He gets the glory, honor, and praise out of my life! It's His sweet-smelling savor of rescue and recovery….

So after being celibate (3 years) and in my season of sanctification, God finally said 'Now I'm ready to present you to your husband. He then allowed me to meet and marry my soul mate Timothy R. Cox. The way God so beautifully orchestrated this was nothing short of a miracle. We met on October 21, 2000, and we became husband and wife THE very next month on November 27th, 2000. We both were attending the same ministry conference in Dallas, TX. I flew from my hometown of Plainview and all the while, Timothy was traveling from Kenly, North Carolina. Now grant it, neither one of us knew each other even existed before our divine connection. Well, it was after service that Saturday evening, and I kept noticing this one extremely handsome, fine brother while walking through and waiting on my family. I simply noted that each time we would pass each other; we'd casually nod or gently wave. Well, come to find out he left the sanctuary and was heading back to North Carolina….. But Holy Spirit stopped him in his tracks and spoke "Go back' and find her. He automatically knew why…. he then found me and we introduced ourselves…. long story short..... THE VERY NEXT MONTH on November 27th we were united in holy matrimony. https://youtu.be/8acKBFVgMi0

Yes, in less than 30 days we knew God had ordained us to be married. In our very first telephone conversation, I KNEW Tim was my husband! How did I know? Well, I'm glad you asked…He had a distinguished sound! No, not in his tone but what he said and prophesied to me. His words sounded like a verbatim of everything God had gently whispered in my spirit. God said, "This is how he's going to talk to you, and this is what he's going to say". As the daughter of Abraham, I had been given divine instructions as I waited on my husband, simply so I would not believe every spirit or fall for any man that tried to pursue me. It didn't matter who you were or how good you looked. I was told "Beloved, believe not every spirit, but try the spirits whether they are of God: because many false prophets are gone out into the world" (1 John 4). If you were not the one, there was no need of wasting my time. Period! I meant business with God and when you mean business with God, He'll mean business with you.

My prayer request was as simple as 1-2-3 but powerful and proved to be effective.
#1 Lord, I want a husband (not a boyfriend, sugar-daddy, or "friend") and he has to love you as much and even MORE than I do! This was because I knew I had a Deuteronomy 6:5 type of love "And thou shalt love the LORD thy God with all thine heart, and with all thy soul, and with all thy might."

#2 He MUST be God-fearing-meaning he had to have great respect and reverence for God as Father.

#3 He must love my girls (6 & 4 yrs old) as though they are his very own (the adoption was finalized in August of 2011). It's so amazing how much the baby girl looks like Tim and my oldest girl favors me. Nobody but God!! We all fit like a hand in a glove.

So yes, on 11/27/2020, Timothy and I will celebrate twenty years of honoring our marriage vows and we strongly adhere to Mathew 19:6; So then, they are no longer two but one flesh. Therefore what God has joined together, let not man separate." (Talking to the husband and the wife).

Women if you are waiting on God for your husband, I highly encourage you to hide yourself in God as Colossians 3:3 reminds us that your life is hidden with Christ in God. If God did it for me, He will do it for YOU! Trust the process! God will lead your husband right to you. Believe God! Seek His face and pray more than you do anything!! Despite what it looks like, I do believe we're in a season of restoration, redemption, and recovery!! But thanks be to God, which giveth us the victory through our Lord Jesus Christ. (1 Corinthians 15:57)

In conclusion; I would say unto everyone who would read this chapter of my life. Get connected with God and stay connected to Him! I would have never been able to save myself from the hell that was prevalent in my life. No rehabilitation program or therapeutic session could have delivered me from such darkness and pain. Only God! He was and He still is the "Sweet Savor of Rescue and Recovery." He is the only reason why I am the "Resilient Woman" that I am today.

Getting to know Shelva Cox

Prophetess Shelva L. Cox was born on October 11, 1972, in Floydada, Texas. She has been married for 20 years to Timothy Ray Cox. She is the proud mother of two beautiful children (Tahja and Kila). Shelva received her education through Hale County Public School System. She graduated in 1991 from Plainview High School. Following graduation; Shelva decided to attend Jarvis Christian College in Hawkins, Texas where she would later receive her Bachelor's Degree in Business and Administration. Shelva has also attended Wilson Technical College, in Wilson, NC, and Grand Canyon University, in Phoenix, AZ. Shelva was saved at the age of 14. She has practically served God all of her life. In the year of 2004, Shelva was called to the ministry. Today she operates in the Office of the Prophet. She serves God's people through the use and application of the prophetic gifts, gifts of healing, miracles, word of knowledge, etc.

Shelva is also a businesswoman. She is the Founder, Owner, and Director of the previously operated Kindred Kare Learning Center which is a Daycare providing service. Shelva also works with the Mansfield Independent Education system as a Substitute Teacher. She supports her husband as Administrator Assistant of Visions of Life Ministries and Counseling Services.

Shelva is a gift to the entire world. She is a dedicated, willing, teachable, and available vessel being used mightily by God for the building of His Kingdom. Her purpose and passion are to "push people past their pain" and point them in the direction of their eternal destiny.

The Sweet Scent of

Tenacity

BY

THE VISIONARY KENDRA C.SIKES

As women, we tend to forget the one key ingredient to seamless victory…..Tenacity.

Many times we are faced with trials and tribulations that at times can cause us to nearly lose sight of our promises and dang near give up on our purpose. In this book, we share different faces, seasons, phases, and lessons that left a fragrance of resilience in our lives.

Here is my story; A story of perseverance. A kind that will have you ready to get up and pursue your dreams and tell Satan he can have your past but not your future.

What is Resilience? It is the capacity to recover quickly from difficulties; toughness.

In my Resilient life, I was given a cross to bear that shaped me into becoming a woman of tenacity. I am a servant of GOD, mother, wife, business owner of multiple brands, ordained minister, and helpmate to a man that also has several brands. Shout out to my support system and love of my life Kenneth D-Lou Sikes. The one thing that gave me victory was learning to become a thriver after dealing with loss, lack, poverty, drug use, abuse, and molestation. Throughout life, I had to understand those things were sent shape and mold me into the woman that I am today.

What is Tenacity? It is persistence, determination, and perseverance.

At a young age, I learned to survive. Not just because my family lived in poverty, but because I felt something deep within telling me I would be successful. I wasn't your normal kid. I didn't play with dolls, I didn't play with hair, I used to play "Business" well, that is what I called it. I remember being in my room with my dad's briefcase dressed in my imaginary pumps and pantsuit giving orders to my employees. No longer paying attention to the pain of deep wombs I suffered being a little girl in a home of chaos. I had to find a way to escape. I did just that… I barricaded the pain in my own desire to be a woman of purpose.

The birthing of Kendra C. Sikes "The Tenacious Go-Getter"

At the age of 12, I had my first job. I was a sales rep for "Drug Free America". My brothers and I sold candy bars in front of stores to earn money. It was then I got a taste of independence. I made nearly $200 a week at 12 years old and I loved the feeling of having my own money. My mom told me that she was proud of me because she noticed maturity in my character as a young black 12-year-old. Those words changed life. I wanted to take care of my mother. I witnessed her most hurtful moments crying after being abused by my dad or stressed because he went MIA after a weeklong binge on Crack Cocaine, leaving her with no car or money. I desired to hear the echo of her asking for 10 dollars in need of a pack of Newport Menthol 100 cigarettes. Being able to provide a few dollars here and there to ease my mom's pain was heaven to me. That feeling gave me an immature motivation because I was only 12. I can still hear my pitch ringing in my ears, "Hi, do you want to buy a candy bar for Drug Free America to keep kids and drugs off the streets? There is also a coupon on the back for a free domino's pizza". The sound of "yes" was like music to my ears and the sound of "no" was even better because that meant that I could ask for a donation and pocket all of the money without the 70/30 split. I was one of the best sellers. I sold 2 or 3 boxes a day. The weekends were my favorite days of the week because I was out grinding and getting a break from all the confusion in our home. Fighting and drinking was normal at the second house on the left of Timberline Dr. I saw lots of things someone my age should not have seen. Although being a young go-getter was part of my life, depression and low self-esteem were another. The little face in the mirror that everyone said was so cute was hurtful to me. I didn't like the way I looked. I allowed myself to assimilate the pernicious words of my school mates. Being bullied for my wide nose and big lips left me feeling less than.

Being introduced to my spiritual side

I didn't grow up in church nor did my parents make attending service repetition. Some summers my dad sent me to spend time with my older sister as they worked during the day. I wasn't in agreement with that because I wanted to make my money, but GOD had a plan for me. Being at my sister's house was my only time to get to know my savior. We had service Wednesday, Friday, and Sunday morning and we were in attendance faithfully. One Sunday morning the presence of GOD hit me strongly. Tears swelled in my eyes and conviction hit my heart. I was then crying out for repentance. Although my walk with GOD didn't last long I still strived to be Holy. At age 12 it's kind of hard living that life, a life of purity and innocence. I remember walking the hallways holding my bible with pride wearing nothing but dresses because a woman wearing pants was blasphemy but I couldn't quite get it right. Something was missing, something I was seeking and I needed to fill that void. Later I found out the void I was missing was the need to feel loved. Looking back over those years now I realize that the people I thought didn't love me had their own issues. I used to blame my mother for everything I went through not realizing she loved me the best she knew how to. She loved me through her own pain. My mom is a strong black woman and did her best to raise 3 children in her circumstances. I just didn't have that revelation back then. Through it, all GOD was there with me. I had many supernatural experiences with GOD even through my pre-teen/teenage years.

I operated in a prophetic anointing and seer anointing not knowing what it was. I would see spirits and demons in our house. My mom was a dedicated bingo player so many times my brothers and I would be left alone for a few hours. Some of those nights my brothers didn't come home on time so it would be just me, the many spirits I saw and felt, and The Holy Spirit. I would at times see demons running from my parents' room to my brother's room and ugly faced demons staring right at me. I was shaken to the inner core. Some of those demons would manifest and pull me across the floor I laid on, while in sleep paralysis. I could see and hear, but I couldn't move or speak. It was then I was introduced to the power of calling the name Jesus. I would be stuck in that state until I gathered up the strength to call out Jesus. Immediately after confessing that powerful name, the demons left and I would be able to wake up.

Demons weren't the only spirits I encountered. I would sometimes be introduced to the anointing GOD placed on my life while laying in bed at night. The Holy Spirit would hit me and I could feel my spirit arising and making me feel as If I were a giant. I could feel my hands, feet, teeth, and body enlarge in the spirit and it would feel as if I was filling up the whole space in the room. I didn't know what it was then. I was clueless to the power I had within.

Satan's attempts to distract me from the purpose

Many young girls and boys are open to the spirit of perversion from things suffered as a child. Perversion is defined as the condition of being perverted or corrupt. The spirit of perversion can be manifested in many ways such as sexual perversions, child abuse, pornography, incest, having a filthy mind, chronic worrying, walking in foolishness, twisting the word of God, evil actions, abortion, having a broken spirit, doctrinal error, and atheism. There was an older teenage girl I saw often during the summer at my sister's house. She was a very attractive young lady and I had no idea that she was interested in me. I was ignorant of homosexuality and lesbianism. I was interested in hanging around a cool, hip, and older teenager and never intending on being forced into sexual activities and being touched with objects and bare hands as well as being taught to perform sexual activities on her. I thought it was normal behavior because as we slept together in the same bed no one ever questioned or was aware of what was going on.

Those activities opened doors to other spirits that affected my teenage/adult years. I had to be delivered from pornography, promiscuous behavior with both men and women, and not valuing myself as a young lady.

Being under the spirit of perversion led me down a dark and dangerous path that nearly ended my life numerous times. If it wasn't for the grace of GOD the Kendra C. Sikes you know today would be in Hell. I know it is harsh to say, but it was my reality before I totally submitted to GOD.

Many times one spiritual will lead to another if you're not freed from the bondage. **Matthew 12:45 NIV Version** "Then it goes and takes with it seven other spirits more wicked than itself. They go in and live there. That person is worse off than before."

Perversion led to me dibbling and dabbling in drugs, love of money, fornication, lust, hatred, unforgiveness, and the list goes on. I had no regard for The Holy Spirit I once knew as a child. It took a young boy in my classroom while studying for my GED to remind me of my purpose. I heard someone say "Ma'am, you will have a ministry for women". Although my spirit agreed to his declaration over my future my flesh was in no rush to stop living a lifestyle I thought was fun. I fell into the schemes of the enemy. It was Satan's plan to keep me drowning in wombs from my childhood. The little broken girl inside of me attracted familiar spirits. I ended up in relations with friends and intimate relationships with vessels the enemy used to destroy me physically and mentally.

Drugs, partying, and alcohol became my scapegoat. I started out only smoking marijuana and drinking here and there to popping pills to a full out cocaine addiction. By this time I already had four kids and in a very abusive relationship. I honestly did not have any plans to quit using, but GOD! He had other plans for me. It is funny how the same things the enemy uses to kill you GOD takes those very things and uses us for his glory. **Psalm 37:23-24 NIV Version** "The Lord makes firm the steps of one who delights in him, though he may stumble, he will not fail."

My Spirit being awakened after an attack on my life

One hot summer night after hanging with some friends and using cocaine from dusk to dawn, I went home to lay down. Something didn't feel right. Most people say when surviving a near-death experience they felt something was off. My spirit attempted to alarm me many times, but I didn't listen. I laid down on my mother's couch, that is where my children and I resided due to being flat out irresponsible with my money. My breathing began to feel shallow and my eyes began to blur. I could feel my heartbeat at an irregular pace. Not knowing if I was just high off some top-grade "FREE" drugs or if I was slowly losing my life. I laid there for a moment and then I could feel a stabbing pain in my chest. With my hand on my chest, I got up, weak in the knees, and all and stumbled my way to the hallway mirror my mom had in the hallway. I looked at my chest and could see my heart appearing as if it was going to pop out at any moment. Ashamed, scared, and paranoid I ran out the front door and ended up in front of my mom's window, just in case if I were going to die, I wanted my mom to find me. I then felt my knees buckle and the only thing I could think to do was scream out "JESUS". I gained a little strength but it lasted only a few seconds. I called out "JESUS" again. I felt my knees buckle the third time and this time I literally felt my spirit leaving my body. I began to fall to the ground. I said, "JESUS, help me! Give me a second chance. Please forgive me". I don't know if you know what's so significant about me calling the name of Jesus 3 times? Jesus rose from the dead on the third day. I immediately felt strength in my body, my heartbeat began to decelerate and I was able to breathe without the shallow feeling. Me calling the name of Jesus 3 times and nothing happening until I called his name the third time was a revelation of the dead being raised. I knew I would serve HIM the rest of my life.

I honestly didn't immediately repent, but I had a fear and reverence for GOD.

The Job Experience

2014 is when I totally submitted to GOD. My now-husband gave his life to Christ and encouraged me to join and I slowly did. Things I used to do I wasn't interested in doing and places I used to go I had no desire to go. I developed a faithful relationship with GOD and wanted the world to know it. I was hungry to know my purpose and what GOD had for me. I can admit me serving GOD was a blessing in my life. I had a favor anointing attached to me that no one could explain. Everything I prayed for was given to me, but it didn't come without a test.

Due to my husband's addiction and many experiences with lack of money we spent many years living with family members, living in hotels, sleeping in the cars just to be with each other because our families had issues. We would get a place to stay and have to move out several months later. We had houses and cars, but never could keep them so we always ended back at square one; having nothing. Our losses always seemed to happen around the same time of the year. You would think we were cursed. Even though all of that I never gave up on GOD. I remained faithful and kept my faith. Sitting in a church service one Sunday evening, I received a word that changed my life. A MOG said GOD told him that I would write books. At that time it clearly seemed as if he missed the mark because I had no interest in writing at all. With doubt in my flesh, my spirit agreed to his words.

Side note: It is important to agree with what confirms in your spirit no matter how imperfect your life may seem. You could be in your sin and GOD will speak to you. Test the spirits that are speaking over your life. When you hear GOD you will know when he is speaking to you. It may not look like it makes sense at the time, but GOD'S timing is perfect. His ways are above our ways. His thoughts are above our thoughts and he has a plan for you according to Jeremiah 29:11. "For I know the plans I have for you," declares the Lord, "plans to prosper you and not to harm you, plans to give you hope and a future." Trust his word and have faith in his timing and he will lead you. "**Trust in the LORD** with all your heart, and do not lean on your own understanding. In all your ways acknowledge him, and he will make straight your paths." Proverbs 3:5.

It was two years after that word I received the unction of the Holy Spirit to write my very first book. Shortly after that, I was given the green light to start a business. GOD normally speaks to me through dreams and visions and I saw myself birthing the business I had been pregnant with since I was 12 years old. Attempting to start my business was very painful but I was determined. We all know when you're getting ready to give birth there are contractions. Those contractions come with a lot of pain and the baby will not be birthed unless you push! Not pushing and preventing the baby from coming out can also cause birth defects. Birth defects can lead to the death of the baby. I want to encourage you to know that No matter where you are in life, whatever you want to do just SHOW UP!!!!

The Birthing of something Great

We moved to Atlanta Georgia after feeling led to start our life and ministry on new soil. We were living with a family we barely knew. Shortly after arriving in Atlanta, we lost our car, and after believing I had a job when we got there that reality was snatched away from me. The Apostle we lived with said GOD told him our time there was up and he should take us to a shelter. I didn't fight it because I knew GOD wouldn't bring us that far to leave us. A door opened for us to move without deposit, but we had no car. I had every reason to give up on my faith, but I didn't. I was determined to fulfill the dream GOD gave me.

The Beginning of something Great Pt. 2

I started my business and all I had was hope, drive, a plan, and most of all FAITH while being broke. Very humbling to me but no one knew the sacrifices I had made to be present that day. I was at the beginning stages of my business and I was broke. I walked 2 miles to the nearest Dunkin donuts just to use wifi to begin to promote my new book coaching business. Multiple of our utilities were cut off. I was going through, but I was determined.

I remember talking to potential clients from Dunkin Donuts on wifi because my phone had been disconnected. I didn't give any excuses. I knew if GOD told me to start this business he would make away. I didn't have a laptop. I had a phone, a notebook, and a pen. (LATER GOD SPOKE TO SOMEONE AND TOLD THEM TO GIVE ME A LAPTOP) Many days I cried but I NEVER gave up. I remember being approached to come to speak at this event as a panelist based on my experience in the business. I didn't understand why they wanted me, but I dust off my doubt and I showed up.

I came in and walked in with confidence, sat up there on the panel, and answered my questions with passion. I was shocked because afterward, so many women wanted to talk to lil ole me.

Why am I sharing this? I want to encourage you to start with what you have even if it's only faith.

I started my publishing company with 0 dollars and faith while overcoming many obstacles and now I am where I am today.

Don't let your current circumstances stop you from showing up. I promise if you just SHOW up, GOD will show out. Write the vision, make it plain! Take step one, GOD will take step 2.

In the midst of my struggles, I pressed past the many attempts to delay my arrival in purpose. I am a living witness that your past doesn't determine your future. If you submit to GOD the enemy will flee. He may come to distract you, but if you hang on to GOD'S word you will win!

My tenacity is the reason I am a CEO of multiple brands, an Investor, Best Selling Author, and midwife to those that have powerful stories in their bellies. As you're reading this book, allow us to speak life into you. Every chapter is proof that no matter what the enemy throws at you, you can stand against the darts of the enemy.

I don't know what you're going through right now. Are you reading this to pump yourself up? Maybe for healing, maybe a business setback, maybe a difficult relationship? Are you scraping the bottom of your soul for the inspiration that you're sure is hiding somewhere? Has your past left you with hidden needles in the haystack of your mind, that you're only now starting to sift through? Or maybe, you're reading this for a friend – someone you love, and your own words don't seem like enough.

Well, take heart, sis. Some of the best minds have distilled some of humanity's best wisdom, just for us. Be inspired, and then inspire others.

There is nothing you cannot overcome! You can too be a RESILIENT WOMAN!

Signed,

A Resilient tenacious woman.-Kendra C. Sikes